CAREER IDEAS for kids who like WRITING

CAREER IDEAS for kids who like WRITING

DIANE LINDSEY REEVES

Illustrations by
NANCY BOND

Checkmark Books®
An imprint of Facts On File, Inc.

CAREER IDEAS FOR KIDS WHO LIKE WRITING

Checkmark Books
An imprint of Facts On File, Inc.
132 West 31st Street
New York NY 10001

Library of Congress Cataloging-in-Publication Data

Reeves, Diane Lindsey, 1959–
Writing / Diane Lindsey Reeves, illustrations by Nancy Bond.
p. cm.—(Career ideas for kids who like)
Includes bibliographical references and index.
Summary: Provides activities to uncover individual traits and abilities, information about careers in writing, description of career planning resources, explanations for personal roadmaps, and profiles of individuals with writing careers.
ISBN 0-8160-3685-3 (HC : alk. paper). — ISBN 0-8160-3691-8 (PB : alk. paper)
1. Authorship—Vocational guidance—Juvenile literature. 2. Creative writing—Vocational guidance—Juvenile literature. 3. Book industry and trade—Vocational guidance—Juvenile literature. [1. Authorship—Vocational guidance. 2. Creative writing—Vocational guidance. 3. Book industry and trade—Vocational guidance. 4. Vocational guidance.] I. Bond, Nancy, ill. II. Title. III. Title: Career ideas for kids who like writing. IV. Series: Reeves, Diane Lindsey, 1959– Career ideas for kids who like.
PN151.R42 1998
808'.02'023—dc21 98-6229

Checkmark Books are available at special discounts when purchased in bulk quantities for businesses, associations, institutions or sales promotions. Please call our Special Sales Department in New York at 212/967-8800 or 800/322-8755.

You can find Facts On File on the World Wide Web at http://www.factsonfile.com

Text and cover design by Smart Graphics
Illustrations by Nancy Bond

This book is printed on acid-free paper.

Printed in the United States of America

MP FOF 10 9 8 7 6

(pbk) 10 9 8 7 6 5

To my parents,
Buford and Barbara Lindsey,
whose love and encouragement
made it possible for me to
pursue my dream
of becoming a writer

CONTENTS

ACKNOWLEDGMENTS

Special thanks to
Marilyn Pollard
for all she added to this book—
the feedback, the great interviews,
and most of all,
the friendship

A million thanks to the people who took the time to share their career stories and provide photos for this book:

Debbie Becker
Chris Chavez
Wayne Crocker
Elizabeth Curtler
Chris Dealy
Paul and Sarah Edwards
Kimberle English
Ann Flower
Tom Giesen
David Hendin
Susan Lingo
Eileen O'Reilly
Sue Rugge
Clara Villarosa
Naomi Wax

Also, special thanks to the design team of Smart Graphics, Nancy Bond, and Cathy Rincon for bringing the Career Ideas for Kids series to life with their creative talent.

Finally, much appreciation and admiration is due to my editor, Nicole Bowen, whose vision and attention to detail increased the quality of this project in many wonderful ways.

MAKE A CHOICE!

You're young. Most of your life is still ahead of you. How are you supposed to know what you want to be when you grow up?

You're right: 10, 11, 12, 13 is a bit young to know exactly what and where and how you're going to do whatever it is you're going to do as an adult. But, it's the perfect time to start making some important discoveries about who you are, what you like to do, and what you do best. It's the ideal time to start thinking about what you *want* to do.

Make a choice! If you get a head start now, you may avoid setbacks and mistakes later on.

When it comes to picking a career, you've basically got two choices.

CHOICE A

Wait until you're in college to start figuring out what you want to do. Even then you still may not decide what's up your alley, so you graduate and jump from job to job still searching for something you really like.

Hey, it could work. It might be fun. Lots of (probably most) people do it this way.

The problem is that if you pick Choice A, you may end up settling for second best. You may miss out on a meaningful education, satisfying work, and the rewards of a focused and well-planned career.

You have another choice to consider.

CHOICE B

Start now figuring out your options and thinking about the things that are most important in your life's work: Serving others? Staying true to your values? Making lots of money? Enjoying your work? Your young years are the perfect time to mess around with different career ideas without messing up your life.

Reading this book is a great idea for kids who choose B. It's a first step toward choosing a career that matches your skills, interests, and lifetime goals. It will help you make a plan for tailoring your junior and high school years to fit your career dreams. To borrow a jingle from the U.S. Army—using this book is a way to discover how to "be all that you can be."

Ready for the challenge of Choice B? If so, read the next section to find out how this book can help start you on your way.

HOW TO USE THIS BOOK

This isn't a book about interesting careers that other people have. It's a book about interesting careers that you can have.

Of course, it won't do you a bit of good to just read this book. To get the whole shebang, you're going to have to jump in with both feet, roll up your sleeves, put on your thinking cap—whatever it takes—to help you do these three things:

- **Discover** what you do best and enjoy the most. (This is the secret ingredient for finding work that's perfect for you.)

- **Explore** ways to match your interests and abilities with career ideas.
- **Experiment** with lots of different ideas until you find the ideal career. (It's like trying on all kinds of hats to see which ones fit!)

Use this book as a road map to some exciting career destinations. Here's what to expect in the chapters that follow.

GET IN GEAR!

First stop: self-discovery. These activities will help you uncover important clues about the special traits and abilities that make you *you*. When you are finished you will have developed a personal Skill Set that will help guide you to career ideas in the next chapter.

TAKE A TRIP!

Next stop: exploration. Cruise down the career idea highway and find out about a variety of career ideas that are especially appropriate for people who like writing. Use the Skill Set chart at the beginning of each entry to match your own interests with those required for success on the job.

MAKE A WRITING DETOUR!

Here's your chance to explore up-and-coming opportunities as a book packager and information broker as well as the tried-and-true routes of editor, librarian, and journalist.

Just when you thought you'd seen it all, here come dozens of interesting writing ideas to add to the career mix. Charge up your career search by learning all you can about some of these opportunities.

DON'T STOP NOW!

Third stop: experimentation. The library, the telephone, a computer, and a mentor—four keys to a successful career planning adventure. Use them well, and before long you'll be on the trail of some hot career ideas.

WHAT'S NEXT?

Make a plan! Chart your course (or at least the next stop) with these career planning road maps. Whether you're moving full steam ahead with a great idea or get slowed down at a yellow light of indecision, these road maps will keep you moving forward toward a great future.

Use a pencil—you're bound to make a detour or two along the way. But, hey, you've got to start somewhere.

HOORAY! YOU DID IT!

Some final rules of the road before sending you off to new adventures.

SOME FUTURE DESTINATIONS

This section lists a few career planning tools you'll want to know about.

You've got a lot of ground to cover in this phase of your career planning journey. Start your engines and get ready for an exciting adventure!

GET IN GEAR!

Career planning is a lifelong journey. There's usually more than one way to get where you're going, and there are often some interesting detours along the way. But, you have to start somewhere. So, rev up and find out all you can about you—one-of-a-kind, specially designed you. That's the first stop on what can be the most exciting trip of your life!

To get started, complete the two exercises described below.

WATCH FOR SIGNS ALONG THE WAY

Road signs help drivers figure out how to get where they want to go. They provide clues about direction, road conditions, and safety. Your career road signs will provide clues about who you are, what you like, and what you do best. These clues can help you decide where to look for the career ideas that are best for you.

Complete the following statements to make them true for you. There are no right or wrong answers. Jot down the response that describes you best. Your answers will provide important clues about career paths you should explore.

Please Note: If this book does not belong to you, write your responses on a separate sheet of paper.

On my last report card, I got the best grade in __________.

On my last report card, I got the worst grade in __________.

I am happiest when __________.

Something I can do for hours without getting bored is __________.

Something that bores me out of my mind is __________.

My favorite class is __________.

My least favorite class is __________.

The one thing I'd like to accomplish with my life is __________.

My favorite thing to do after school is __________.

My least favorite thing to do after school is __________.

Something I'm really good at is __________.

Something that is really tough for me to do is __________.

My favorite adult person is __________ because __________.

When I grow up __________.

The kinds of books I like to read are about __________.

The kinds of videos I like to watch are about __________.

GET SOME DIRECTION

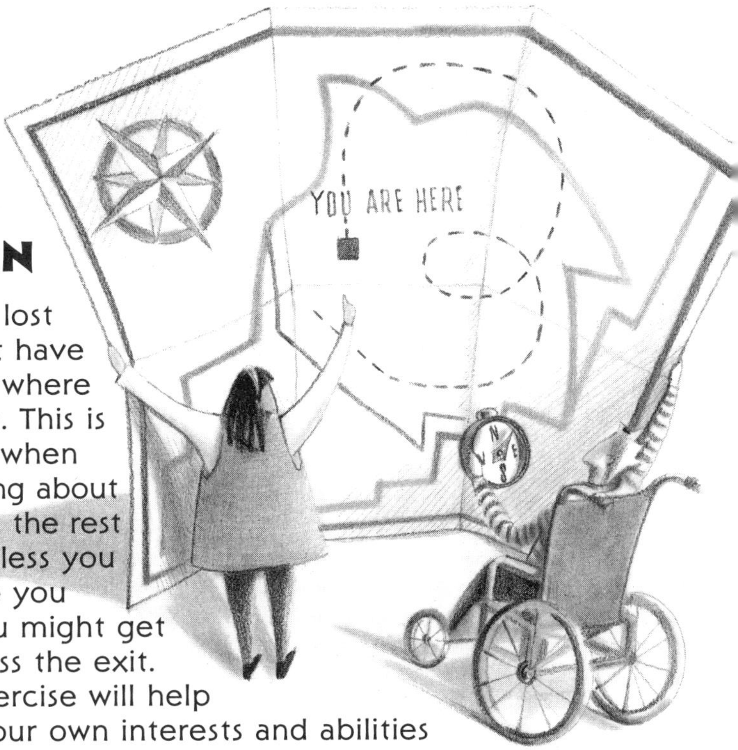

It's easy to get lost when you don't have a good idea of where you want to go. This is especially true when you start thinking about what to do with the rest of your life. Unless you focus on where you want to go, you might get lost or even miss the exit. This second exercise will help you connect your own interests and abilities with a whole world of career opportunities.

Mark the activities that you enjoy doing or would enjoy doing if you had the chance. Be picky. Don't mark ideas that you wish you would do, mark only those that you would really do. For instance, if the idea of skydiving sounds appealing, but you'd never do it because you are terrified of heights, don't mark it.

Please Note: If this book does not belong to you, write your responses on a separate sheet of paper.

❑ 1. Rescue a cat stuck in a tree
❑ 2. Visit the pet store every time you go to the mall
❑ 3. Paint a mural on the cafeteria wall
❑ 4. Run for student council
❑ 5. Send e-mail to a "pen pal" in another state
❑ 6. Survey your classmates to find out what they do after school
❑ 7. Try out for the school play
❑ 8. Dissect a frog and identify the different organs
❑ 9. Play baseball, soccer, football, or _________ (fill in your favorite sport)

❑ 10. Talk on the phone to just about anyone who will talk back
❑ 11. Try foods from all over the world—Thailand, Poland, Japan, etc.
❑ 12. Write poems about things that are happening in your life
❑ 13. Create a really scary haunted house to take your friends through on Halloween
❑ 14. Recycle all your family's trash
❑ 15. Bake a cake and decorate it for your best friend's birthday
❑ 16. Sell enough advertisements for the school yearbook to win a trip to Walt Disney World
❑ 17. Simulate an imaginary flight through space on your computer screen
❑ 18. Build model airplanes, boats, doll houses, or anything from kits
❑ 19. Teach your friends a new dance routine
❑ 20. Watch the stars come out at night and see how many constellations you can find
❑ 21. Watch baseball, soccer, football, or _____ (fill in your favorite sport) on TV
❑ 22. Give a speech in front of the entire school
❑ 23. Plan the class field trip to Washington, D.C.
❑ 24. Read everything in sight, including the back of the cereal box
❑ 25. Figure out "who dunnit" in a mystery story
❑ 26. Take in stray or hurt animals
❑ 27. Make a poster announcing the school football game
❑ 28. Think up a new way to make the lunch line move faster and explain it to the cafeteria staff
❑ 29. Put together a multimedia show for a school assembly using music and lots of pictures and graphics
❑ 30. Invest your allowance in the stock market and keep track of how it does
❑ 31. Go to the ballet or opera every time you get the chance
❑ 32. Do experiments with a chemistry set
❑ 33. Keep score at your sister's Little League game

- ❏ 34. Use lots of funny voices when reading stories to children
- ❏ 35. Ride on airplanes, trains, boats—anything that moves
- ❏ 36. Interview the new exchange student for an article in the school newspaper
- ❏ 37. Build your own treehouse
- ❏ 38. Help clean up a waste site in your neighborhood
- ❏ 39. Visit an art museum and pick out your favorite painting
- ❏ 40. Play Monopoly® in an all-night championship challenge
- ❏ 41. Make a chart on the computer to show how much soda students buy from the school vending machines each week
- ❏ 42. Keep track of how much your team earns to buy new uniforms
- ❏ 43. Play an instrument in the school band or orchestra
- ❏ 44. Put together a 1,000-piece puzzle
- ❏ 45. Write stories about sports for the school newspaper
- ❏ 46. Listen to other people talk about their problems
- ❏ 47. Imagine yourself in exotic places
- ❏ 48. Hang around bookstores and libraries
- ❏ 49. Play harmless practical jokes on April Fools' Day

- ❑ 50. Join the 4-H club at your school
- ❑ 51. Take photographs at the school talent show
- ❑ 52. Make money by setting up your own business—paper route, lemonade stand, etc.
- ❑ 53. Create an imaginary city using a computer
- ❑ 54. Do 3-D puzzles
- ❑ 55. Keep track of the top 10 songs of the week
- ❑ 56. Train your dog to do tricks
- ❑ 57. Make play-by-play announcements at the school football game
- ❑ 58. Answer the phones during a telethon to raise money for orphans
- ❑ 59. Be an exchange student in another country
- ❑ 60. Write down all your secret thoughts and favorite sayings in a journal
- ❑ 61. Jump out of an airplane (with a parachute, of course)
- ❑ 62. Plant and grow a garden in your backyard (or windowsill)
- ❑ 63. Use a video camera to make your own movies
- ❑ 64. Get your friends together to help clean up your town after a hurricane
- ❑ 65. Spend your summer at a computer camp learning lots of new computer programs

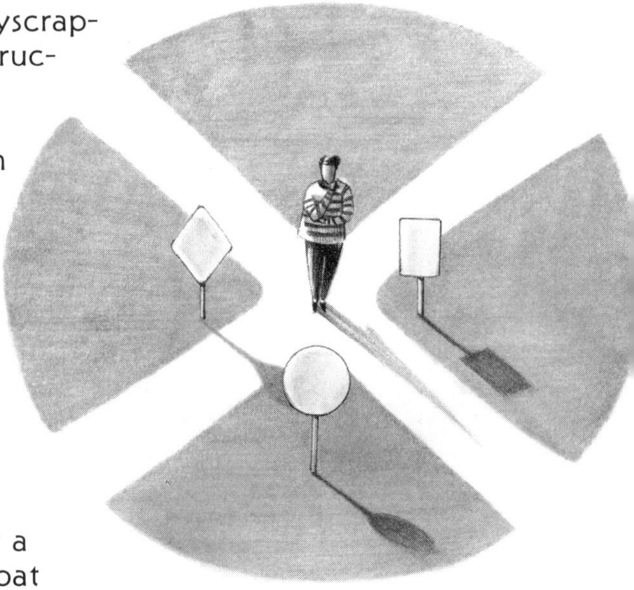

- ❑ 66. Build bridges, skyscrapers, and other structures out of LEGO®s
- ❑ 67. Plan a concert in the park for little kids
- ❑ 68. Collect different kinds of rocks
- ❑ 69. Help plan a sports tournament
- ❑ 70. Be DJ for the school dance
- ❑ 71. Learn how to fly a plane or sail a boat
- ❑ 72. Write funny captions for pictures in the school yearbook
- ❑ 73. Scuba dive to search for buried treasure
- ❑ 74. Recognize and name several different breeds of cats, dogs, and other animals
- ❑ 75. Sketch pictures of your friends
- ❑ 76. Pick out neat stuff to sell at the school store
- ❑ 77. Answer your classmates' questions about how to use the computer
- ❑ 78. Draw a map showing how to get to your house from school
- ❑ 79. Make up new words to your favorite songs
- ❑ 80. Take a hike and name the different kinds of trees, birds, or flowers
- ❑ 81. Referee intramural basketball games
- ❑ 82. Join the school debate team
- ❑ 83. Make a poster with postcards from all the places you went on your summer vacation
- ❑ 84. Write down stories that your grandparents tell you about when they were young

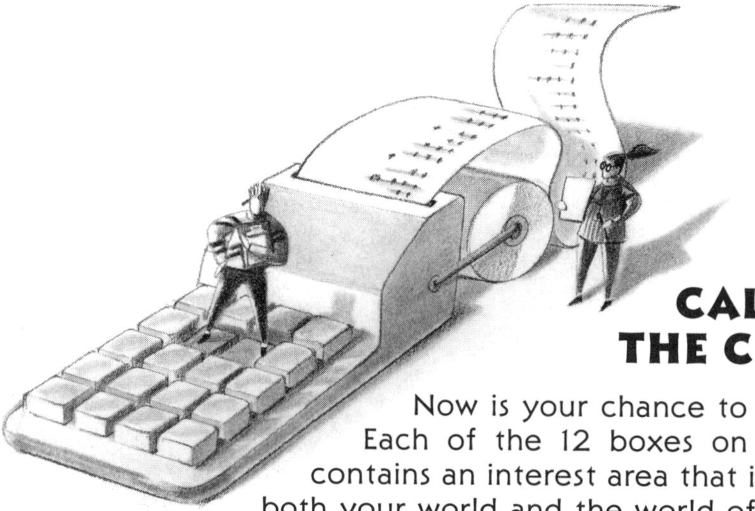

CALCULATE THE CLUES

Now is your chance to add it all up. Each of the 12 boxes on these pages contains an interest area that is common to both your world and the world of work. Follow these directions to discover your personal Skill Set:

1. Find all of the numbers that you checked on pages 9–13 in the boxes below and X them. Work your way all the way through number 84.
2. Go back and count the Xs marked for each interest area. Write that number in the space that says "total."
3. Find the interest area with the highest total and put a number one in the "Rank" blank of that box. Repeat this process for the next two highest scoring areas. Rank the second highest as number two and the third highest as number three.
4. If you have more than three strong areas, choose the three that are most important and interesting to you.

Remember: If this book does not belong to you, write your responses on a separate sheet of paper.

ADVENTURE

❏ 1
❏ 13
❏ 25
❏ 37
❏ 49
❏ 61
❏ 73
Total: ____
Rank: ____

ANIMALS & NATURE

❏ 2
❏ 14
❏ 26
❏ 38
❏ 50
❏ 62
❏ 74
Total: ____
Rank: ____

ART

❏ 3
❏ 15
❏ 27
❏ 39
❏ 51
❏ 63
❏ 75
Total: ____
Rank: ____

BUSINESS

- ❑ 4
- ❑ 16
- ❑ 28
- ❑ 40
- ❑ 52
- ❑ 64
- ❑ 76

Total: ______
Rank: ______

COMPUTERS

- ❑ 5
- ❑ 17
- ❑ 29
- ❑ 41
- ❑ 53
- ❑ 65
- ❑ 77

Total: ______
Rank: ______

MATH

- ❑ 6
- ❑ 18
- ❑ 30
- ❑ 42
- ❑ 54
- ❑ 66
- ❑ 78

Total: ______
Rank: ______

MUSIC/DANCE

- ❑ 7
- ❑ 19
- ❑ 31
- ❑ 43
- ❑ 55
- ❑ 67
- ❑ 79

Total: ______
Rank: ______

SCIENCE

- ❑ 8
- ❑ 20
- ❑ 32
- ❑ 44
- ❑ 56
- ❑ 68
- ❑ 80

Total: ______
Rank: ______

SPORTS

- ❑ 9
- ❑ 21
- ❑ 33
- ❑ 45
- ❑ 57
- ❑ 69
- ❑ 81

Total: ______
Rank: ______

TALKING

- ❑ 10
- ❑ 22
- ❑ 34
- ❑ 46
- ❑ 58
- ❑ 70
- ❑ 82

Total: ______
Rank: ______

TRAVEL

- ❑ 11
- ❑ 23
- ❑ 35
- ❑ 47
- ❑ 59
- ❑ 71
- ❑ 83

Total: ______
Rank: ______

WRITING

- ❑ 12
- ❑ 24
- ❑ 36
- ❑ 48
- ❑ 60
- ❑ 72
- ❑ 84

Total: ______
Rank: ______

What are your top three interest areas? List them here (or on a separate piece of paper).

1. ______________________________

2. ______________________________

3. ______________________________

This is your personal Skill Set and provides important clues about the kinds of work you're most likely to enjoy. Remember it and look for career ideas with a skill set that matches yours most closely.

TAKE A TRIP!

Cruise down the career idea highway and enjoy in-depth profiles of some of the interesting options in this field. Keep in mind all that you've discovered about yourself so far. Find the careers that match your own Skill Set first. After that, keep on trucking through the other ideas—exploration is the name of this game.

Writing careers are based on exceptionally good communication skills. Keep in mind that writing and talking skills tend to go hand in hand (sort of like shoes and socks). If you're going to make your living as a communicator, make sure to work on both sides of the communication process.

Meanwhile, as you read about the following careers, imagine yourself doing each job and ask yourself the following questions:

- Would I like it?
- Would I be good at it?
- Is it the stuff my career dreams are made of?

If so, make a quick exit to explore what it involves, try it out, check it out, and get acquainted!

Buckle up and enjoy the trip!

A NOTE ON WEBSITES

Internet sites tend to move around the Web a bit. If you have trouble finding a particular site, use an Internet browser to find a specific website or type of information.

Advertising Copywriter

SKILL SET
- ✔ ART
- ✔ BUSINESS
- ✔ WRITING

SHORTCUTS

GO billboard hunting to see how copywriters make a few choice words pay off in sky-high signs.

READ advertisements in magazines and newspapers to see copywriters' work in print.

TRY writing an ad to promote the best things about your school.

WHAT IS AN ADVERTISING COPYWRITER?

Believe it or not, you make many decisions under the influence of advertising copywriters. Choices about the brand of clothes you wear, the fast food you eat, the movies you watch, and the games you play, as well as many other decisions, are sometimes the direct result of effective advertising. Copywriters write the words that accompany advertisements, commercials, newspaper and magazine articles, and other sales materials. Good copy (advertising and publishing lingo for the text) informs, educates, entertains, and sells—often in fewer than 10 words.

The copywriter is a vital part of an advertising team that links businesses and their products to consumers and their pocketbooks. Bottom line: Copywriting is salesmanship. Copywriters attempt to persuade consumers to buy a particular product or brand of product. According to the American Association of Advertising Agencies, copywriting is art and science, show business and just plain business, all rolled into one.

Effective copywriters know their words and know how to use them. Quite often, the deadlines are tight, and a copywriter has to come up with a variety of clever and creative ideas quickly. In addition to having outstanding writing skills, a copywriter has to understand people and what motivates them to make purchasing decisions. They also have to understand business and

effective ways to help businesses introduce products and services to the marketplace.

Copywriters work in advertising agencies of all sizes, including everything from a one-person operation to an international corporation that employs thousands of people. They often work for nonprofit organizations as well as television and radio stations, newspapers, and magazines. Experienced copywriters with good contacts often find success as freelancers, which means they work on their own for a variety of clients. Since virtually every business in the world requires advertisement services of one kind or another, the career prospects for talented copywriters are extremely good.

Technically speaking, a college degree isn't necessarily required to become a copywriter; however, in the real scheme of things, a college degree is recommended. Most of the better ad agencies look for a solid background (and college degree) in areas such as English, journalism, mass communication, advertising, marketing, or public relations.

Even more important than a degree is a proven ability to write good copy. Copywriters sell their skills with a portfolio full of creative writing samples. Samples can reflect paid work developed for a client or company as well as ideas developed for classes or for practice. It is even acceptable to develop samples by starting with an existing ad campaign and adding one's own twist to it, as long as the ideas are original and very good.

Copywriting can be an important first step toward other kinds of writing or the answer to a lucrative long-term career.

It really depends on a copywriter's talent and goals. If creative writing in a fast-paced business environment appeals to you, take the advice of one successful copywriter and just do it!

TRY IT OUT

MAKING THE GRADE

To do this first activity, you'll need these items: a notebook, a stack of magazines, some scissors, tape or glue, plain paper, and something to write with. To begin, thumb through some magazines and tear out any advertisements that you find. Tape or glue each ad to a piece of paper. Make three piles according to how you rate each ad. Put the A+ work in one pile. Put the C+ (adequate but sort of ho-hum) ads in another pile. Finally put the worst, poorly crafted ads in a spot for the grade F work.

Now, start with the C+ pile and rework the ads so that they earn a spot in the A+ pile. Keep at it until you come up with some really creative ideas. Do the same for all the ads that flunked. When you've finished, you'll have the beginnings of your professional portfolio.

GET THE INSIDE SCOOP

Copywriters everywhere stay current with what's going on in the industry by reading two magazines: *Advertising Age* and *ADWEEK*. Find copies of these at your local library or request sample copies of *Advertising Age* from Crain Communications, 220 East 42nd Street, New York, New York 10017, and of *ADWEEK* at 1515 Broadway, New York, New York 10036. When you read them, pay attention to what various agencies are doing. Someday you may find yourself employed by one of those companies you read about.

ON-LINE ADS

When it comes to advertising, the Internet is one of the hottest spots in town. Not only can you find helpful information about the profession itself, you can also find literally millions of examples of really creative advertising ideas. Here are a few ways to start your Internet hunt.

- **Check out the work of freelance copywriters.** Use an Internet web browser such as Yahoo and run a search for *copywriters.* Browse through the various sites, and find out how the professionals sell themselves. One interesting site for future copywriters can be found at http://www.copywriting.com. Here you'll find a variety of articles sharing the secrets of good copywriting. Along those same lines is a site for business writers at http://www.martketingmatters.com.
- **Run another search on advertising careers.** Type in *advertising careers;* the results will direct you to a mind-boggling array of resources. Take some time to browse through a number of sites as a way of getting better acquainted with both the industry and the opportunities.
- **Find out how your favorite companies promote themselves on the Internet.** Most of the major names in clothes, food, music, and entertainment host their own Internet sites. Use a web browser to find them. A helpful hint is that most of the brand-name companies simply use their name as the web address. Here are a few examples to get you started:

  http://www.mcdonalds.com
  http://www.fritolay.com
  http://www.pepsi.com

CHECK IT OUT

Advertising Club of New York
155 East 55th Street,
Suite 202
New York, New York 10022

Advertising Research Foundation
641 Lexington Avenue
New York, New York 10022

Advertising Women of New York, Inc.
153 East 57th Street
New York, New York 10022

Affiliated Advertising Agencies International
2280 South Zanadu Way
Aurora, Colorado 80014

American Advertising Federation
1101 Vermont Avenue NW, Suite 500
Washington, D.C. 20005

American Association of Advertising Agencies
666 Third Avenue
New York, New York 10017

Copywriters Council of America
Linick Building 102
7 Putter Lane
Middle Island, New York 11953-0102

GET ACQUAINTED

Chris Dealy, Advertising Copywriter

CAREER PATH

CHILDHOOD ASPIRATION: To be an actor and a professional soccer player.

FIRST JOB: Dishwasher for Swenson's Ice Cream Parlor.

CURRENT JOB: Copywriter for advertising agency, actor in television commercials, and performer with an improvisational comedy group.

SOCCER WAS HIS FIRST LOVE

Chris Dealy grew up and graduated from high school in Washington, D.C. He was a star soccer player in high school and was looking forward to receiving a sports scholarship from a major college. Unfortunately, during his senior year, he broke his back while playing soccer, and his dream of a scholarship from a major college came to an end.

LIFE GOES ON

Dealy did however receive a scholarship from Denison University, a small school in Granville, Ohio, where he continued playing soccer. He spent his junior year in Italy studying and playing soccer. He graduated from Denison with majors in English and creative writing.

FROM THE BUCKEYE STATE TO THE ROCKIES

The two big questions facing any new college graduate are where to go and what to do. Since his girlfriend lived in a Colorado ski town both questions were settled rather quickly. Dealy moved to Breckenridge, Colorado, where he became a self-described ski bum. It was fun for a while, but he eventually reached a point at which he wanted to put to use his college education.

He then moved to New York City, where he worked with a public relations firm. It didn't take long to discover that the Big Apple was just not the place for him. A move to Washington, D.C., followed. There, he taught creative writing and physical education in an elementary school.

BACK TO THE DRAWING BOARD AND INTO THE LIMELIGHT

Dealy taught for a year, but he still wasn't satisfied that he'd found the right career spot. So he returned to Denver and went to work as an intern in an advertising agency. The internship developed into a full-time job writing advertising copy. He now writes print, television, and radio commercials for major national clients. The agency where Dealy works is very community-spirited and does a lot of pro bono (that means "free") work for good causes. This gives Dealy a welcome opportunity to work with cultural and arts organizations in Colorado.

Through this connection Dealy became closely involved in the theater community. Responding to his childhood desire to be an actor, Dealy enrolled in an improvisational acting class and found that he had a talent for performing. He now does five shows a week with a comedy improvisational theater troupe.

GETTING IT ALL TOGETHER

Besides his advertising and comedy work, Dealy uses his talents as an actor in radio and television commercials. He does commercials for such clients as State Farm Insurance, National Car Rental Company, Taco John's, and PBS (the Public Broadcasting System). All together, his writing, performing, and acting combine to make the most of his talents and education.

WORDS OF WISDOM FOR FUTURE COPYWRITERS

Dealy admits to taking a few detours along his career path; however, he is quick to point out that everything he did helped prepare him for what he's doing now. He took a roundabout route for reaching this career destination, but he is now making a good living as a writer. And he loves his extracurricular work as a performer.

Dealy's advice for aspiring copywriters:

- Don't be too hard on yourself.
- Do what you like to do until you don't like doing it anymore.
- Get a well-rounded education and participate in school activities that involve writing—the school newspaper, yearbook, etc.
- Have a keen sense of curiosity and be creative in all you do.

It may take a few different turns to get where you want to be. Just follow your dream, no matter how many setbacks there might be.

Author

SKILL SET

- ✔ ADVENTURE
- ✔ TALKING
- ✔ WRITING

SHORTCUTS

GO visit the website of Oprah Winfrey's book-of-the-month club (http://www.oprah.com). See for yourself how this well-respected celebrity has made overnight sensations out of books that might have otherwise gone unnoticed.

READ *Writers on Writing for Young Adults* by Pamela Barron (Detroit: Omni Graphics, 1991).

TRY keeping track of the best-seller list each week, both fiction and nonfiction, to see what's hot.

WHAT IS AN AUTHOR?

In the most literal sense, anyone who sits down and puts enough words on paper to compose a book is an author. Having readers, or an audience of people who will pay for the opportunity to read that book, is the one very significant detail that separates the wanna-bes from the professionals.

It's quite typical for people to associate being an author with writing novels of one kind or another. It's true that some fiction book authors make a sizable income writing best-selling novels. There are a number of authors who make frequent appearances on best-seller lists. A fortunate few even see their books made into Hollywood movies. These examples of success make writing appear quite glamorous and exciting; however, it can be misleading. The fact of the matter is that very few authors reach this level of success. Face it. There are about 15 slots on the *New York Times* fiction best-seller list. Multiply that by 52 weeks each year and compare the results with the 40,000-plus books that are published every year in the United States. No matter how you figure it, writing a novel is not a sure-fire way to get rich quick.

That is not to say that writing fiction cannot be a rewarding and worthwhile way to make a living as a writer. There are many successful fiction writers who make a comfortable living without all the fanfare of the best-seller lists. These authors tend to specialize in a particular genre, or category, of book, such as mystery, romance, Western, and science fiction, or in writing for a particular audience, such as children or young adults. The secret to success in this area is understanding the interests of a particular audience and writing books that audience will enjoy reading.

Writing fiction is just one way to earn a living as a writer. Nonfiction books offer an immensely broad and interesting arena for talented writers. Nonfiction books run the gamut from sports trivia and cookbooks to travel guides and school textbooks. Nonfiction writers tend to specialize in fields in which they have some expertise or interest. Business, science, education, and computers are some of the areas that a nonfiction writer might focus on.

Surprising as it may seem, nonfiction book authors can often earn significantly more income than fiction book authors. This is because the "shelf life" of a fiction book is often quite short.

Fiction books generally have a very brief window of opportunity to sell—as short as a few weeks and usually not much longer than a year. Those that don't catch on quickly are replaced by the constant flow of new titles. On the other hand, a nonfiction book with a well-defined audience and purpose can continue to sell over any number of years. As long as the book continues to sell, the author continues to earn royalties (a percentage of the price of each book sold, which is paid to the author).

Whether they specialize in fiction or nonfiction, some of the most successful authors are those who find ways to combine their writing with other income-producing activities. Quite often these activities are directly related to their writing and involve public speaking of one sort or another. Teaching college courses or workshops, speaking at conferences and business meetings, and producing audio training materials are just a few of the more common ways that authors supplement their incomes.

As is often the case, there is more than one route to becoming an author. Some people pursue college degrees in journalism or English. Others have degrees in a particular specialty such as business, science, or education, and they write books related to that particular field. Still others find that their educational background has no link whatsoever to what they write. Instead, they write from their own life experiences or observations. Regardless of the educational route an author chooses, he or she must possess three key skills: the ability to write, a steady flow of good ideas, and the self-discipline to actually sit down and write a good book.

TRY IT OUT

WRITE ON!

The only way to become a writer is to write. Of course, you'll want to take all the creative writing courses that you can and take extra care with every term paper you are assigned. The school newspaper and yearbook staff are good places to get your work in print for the first time. All of these approaches will help you hone your skills as a writer.

DEAR DIARY

Keeping a diary or journal is a great way to practice your writing skills. Not only does it give you a chance to record thoughts and observations about life as you see it, but it also helps you develop the self-discipline of writing regularly. Buy yourself a nice notebook or journal. Make yourself write something in it every day.

Your daily contributions can be as varied as your days. One day you might think through a sticky personal problem on paper, and another day you might record a funny joke you heard or an interesting new word. It's your life and your journal—make the most of it.

IDEAS IN A SHOEBOX

Ideas are to a writer, as water is to a well: Without plenty of good ideas, a writer is about as useful as a dried-up well. The good news is that generating ideas is habit forming—one good idea brings another. Once you keep the door open in your mind, you'll find ideas popping up in the most unlikely places—while you're in the shower, just before you nod off to sleep, or when you are trying to listen to a boring lecture at school.

Just don't let any idea go unrecognized. Jot down your idea on anything that's handy, the back of a napkin, a scrap of paper, even the back of your hand will do until you have a chance to transfer the idea to something a bit more permanent. Keep all your ideas in a special place. Sometime those little "seeds" of ideas may grow into a best-selling book.

MEET THE AUTHOR

If you live anywhere near a good-sized bookstore, you may have the opportunity to meet a steady flow of authors. Bookstores host author signings and readings and other special events to boost sales and introduce the buying public to the interesting people behind the latest books. Call the bookstore for a calendar of events or keep tabs on what's happening in local literary circles by reading the book section of the Sunday newspaper.

The Internet is another place to meet even the most famous authors. Some well-known authors host their own websites. If you have a favorite author, use a web browser to run a search on his or her name and see what you find. In addition, check out some of the following Internet bookstores and sit in on some of their on-line chats.

http://www.amazon.com
http://www.barnesandnoble.com
http://www.borders.com

CHECK IT OUT

Academy of American Poets
584 Broadway, Suite 1208
New York, New York 10012

American Black Writers Association
P.O. Box 10548
Marina del Rey, California 90245

American Medical Writers Association
9650 Rockville Pike
Bethesda, Maryland 20814-3998

American Society of Journalists and Authors
1501 Broadway, Suite 302
New York, New York 10036

Authors Guild
234 West 44th Street
New York, New York 10036

Authors League of America, Inc.
330 West 42nd Street
New York, New York 10036

Education Writers Association
1331 H Street NW, Suite 307
Washington, D.C. 20036

National Writers Association
1450 South Havana, Suite 424
Aurora, Colorado 80012

Romance Writers of America
13700 Veteran Memorial Drive, Suite 315
Houston, Texas 77014

Science-Fiction Fantasy Writers of America
5 Winding Brook Drive, Suite 1B
Guilderland, New York 12084

Society of American Travel Writers
4101 Lake Boone Trail, Suite 201
Raleigh, North Carolina 27606

Society of Children's Book Writers and Illustrators
22736 Vanowen Street, Suite 106
West Hills, California 90048

GET ACQUAINTED

Paul and Sarah Edwards,
Authors

CAREER PATH

CHILDHOOD ASPIRATION: Paul wanted to go into politics and to write a book. Sarah always wanted to write a book.

FIRST JOB: Sarah's first job was working at a city recreation center in a park. Paul's was delivering a downtown business newspaper.

CURRENT JOB: Authors; together they have written eight books.

DIFFERENT PATHS

Paul and Sarah Edwards both graduated from the University of Missouri. That's where they met and began their lifelong partnership. Paul "took his mother's advice" and went on to law school and became a lawyer. After graduation, Sarah thought she wanted to be a teacher. Her experiences as a student teacher changed her mind; she decided the teaching field was not for her. She worked for a short time at an insurance company. She then found what she says was a fabulous job with the Head Start program in Kansas City.

NO LONGER AN OPTION

Paul and Sarah got married. After giving birth to their son, Sarah found the long hours and busy travel schedule unfavorable while rearing a child. She returned to school, obtaining a master's degree in social work. This allowed her to open a private psychotherapy practice in her home.

FROM LAW INTO POLITICS

Meanwhile, Paul was practicing law and not enjoying it very much. He decided to enter the political arena. He served as coordinator of intergovernmental relations for a county. He then went to work as an urban specialist for a nonprofit agency. Another career change took him into political consulting (running other people's campaigns), which he did for several years.

A CHANGE OF FOCUS

The Edwardses were still searching for a way to do something in life that would be meaningful to both themselves and to others. The two of them started a business videotaping people in order to teach them how to present themselves. They were excellent trainers, but the void was still there. They resolved to find something that they could do together from home, that would be trendy, and that would help other people find their mission in life. That's how their first book came about.

IN THE RIGHT PLACE AT THE RIGHT TIME

During the early 1980s, more and more people were considering changes in careers. And many of those changes involved home-based careers or businesses. The Edwardses took advantage of the trend. They wrote and published their first book, *Working from Home* (it took five years to write and get published). It's now in its fourth edition. They also conducted workshops across the country, teaching people the basics of working from home.

PREACHING WHAT THEY PRACTICE

The Edwardses have written a total of eight books and plan to have 13 books on the market by the year 2000. Other titles include *Getting Business to Come to You, Secrets of Self-Employment, The Best Home Businesses for the 90s, Making Money with Your Computer at Home, Finding Your Perfect Work, Teaming Up,* and *Home Businesses You Can*

Buy. They, indeed, have become the "gurus" for those who wish to learn about working from home successfully.

A HARD LESSON LEARNED

When the Edwardses first began searching for a publisher, they were assigned an editor who told them that they didn't write well. In response, they hired a writer who had written some 40 books. This writer was told by the same editor that he couldn't write either. The Edwardses then wrote an article for a major magazine and were told by the magazine editor that the writing was great. They then went back to the publishing house, met with someone else, got a new editor, and were on their way.

Rejection can take many forms and be difficult to accept, but it's an experience many writers will have. The Edwardses could have believed that first editor and just given up. But, they are really glad that they didn't. There will always be people who will try to hold you back. But there are many more who will give support and guidance. Seek those people out and persevere. Remember that it is worth taking a few knocks to follow your dream.

WRITE, WRITE, WRITE

The Edwardses' advice for would-be writers is to start writing at an early age. Keep a journal. Write about your experiences—things that you notice are different or funny. Record your observations. And an important part of writing (as painful as it might be) is to share your writing with others. Not everyone will like what you write, but you will be able to connect with some people. Get other people's perspectives. Find out if people are getting your message.

Book Packager

SKILL SET

- ✔ BUSINESS
- ✔ TALKING
- ✔ WRITING

SHORTCUTS

GO visit a bookstore and remember that every book on the shelves started with someone's idea.

READ books in all types of genres (categories). How about a biography, a mystery, or even a popular self-help book?

TRY making a list of all the different kinds of books you can think of—fiction and nonfiction.

WHAT IS A BOOK PACKAGER?

Book packagers, or producers as they are sometimes called, are a new breed of publishing professionals. Assuming some of the responsibilities of literary agent, writer, editor, designer, and printer, book packagers take good ideas and turn them into marketable books. An especially unique feature about many book packagers is that instead of hiring full-time staffs, they put together "virtual" publishing teams that are tailor-made for specific projects. These "dream teams" tend to be small and versatile, with one person often assuming responsibility for more than one aspect of the project.

Book packagers typically handle all, or most of, the steps of making books. They, or members of their team, may write and edit the book itself, design and illustrate the cover and pages, and prepare the materials for the printer. In addition, they must sell the concept to a publisher and negotiate the terms of the partnership. Sometimes they are also asked to develop strategies for marketing the book. Book packagers tend to use the latest technology, which allows them to produce top-quality books quickly and efficiently.

The one thing that most books packagers don't do that traditional publishers do is sell books. Instead, they sell the entire concept, or "package," to publishers who handle all the marketing and distributing tasks. In order to succeed in this field, book packagers must know the kinds of books that specific publishers like and create projects that will enhance a publisher's list of books. Most book packagers work with a variety of publishing houses, so the matchmaking can be quite a challenge.

The result can be a win-win situation for both the packager and the publisher. Publishers win by saving time and money over what it would take to manage and produce the same books in-house. Working with packagers allows them to publish more titles in less time and with less effort than if they did it themselves. With so much of the time-consuming process of creating new books in other capable hands, the publishers can focus on building a solid list of books and devote their efforts to other aspects of the publishing process.

Book packagers win in the same two ways: time and money. By turning the expensive and time-consuming marketing and distributing tasks over to publishing houses, they can focus their efforts on what they do best—producing books. By limiting their focus in this way, they are able to respond quickly to new

trends and opportunities, which is a very good thing in the competitive world of publishing.

Because book packaging is rather new, it isn't a field that requires a specific type of education or training. So far, book packagers tend to be literary-minded entrepreneurs or people with experience in other aspects of the book industry. To prepare yourself for a career in this field, you'll want a strong background in one or more of the following areas: freelance writing or journalism, graphic design or commercial art, editing, or project management. After securing the necessary eduation, you might consider working for a traditional publisher to get a feel for the industry.

Although there are few guarantees in any profession, the future for book packagers looks good. Multimedia and on-line projects are especially promising areas for talented book packagers. Writers willing to ride the wave of the future may find some challenging opportunities in this profession.

TRY IT OUT

GO WITH WHAT YOU KNOW

Writers are often advised to write what they know. That means to write about subjects that are familiar and interesting to them. This isn't bad advice for book packagers either.

What are you most interested in? Sports? Travel? Fashion? Food? Think of some of your favorite interests and come up with several ideas for books that you'd enjoy reading. Make a list of your ideas. When you've come up with a dozen or more ideas, visit the library or a big bookstore and see if there are similar books like the ones you have in mind. If you find similar books, think of ways to give yours a different twist.

DO SOME COMPARISON SHOPPING

According to the American Book Producers Association, some of their members are responsible for an impressive assortment of books currently on the market. Find some of the books that are listed below.

Desaulniers, Marcel. *Death by Chocolate.* New York: St. Martin's Press, 1996.

Ferrand, Phil. *The Nitpicker's Guide for Next Generation Trekkers.* New York: Dell, 1995.

Monteleone, John J. *The Louisville Slugger Ultimate Book of Hitting.* New York: Henry Holt, 1997.
The New York Public Library Desk Reference. New York: Macmillan, 1996.
Penn, W. S. *The Telling of the World: Native American Stories and Art.* New York: Stewart, Tabor & Chang, 1996.
Sehlinger, Bob. *Unofficial Guide to Walt Disney World.* New York: Prentice Hall, 1997.
Thomas, Bob. *Disney's Art of Animation.* New York: Hyperion, 1992.

Book packagers also get involved in producing entire series of books for publishers. New Kids on the Block and Goosebumps are two successful series for young readers that were produced by book packagers. Here are a few (of the many) books from each series to look for.

New Kids on the Block

McEvoy, Seth. *Between Brothers.* New York: Pocket Books, 1991.
———. *Block Party.* New York: Pocket Books, 1991.
———. *On Tour.* New York: Pocket Books, 1991.

Goosebumps

Stine, R. L. *Bad Hare Day.* New York: Scholastic, 1997.
———. *The Blob That Ate Everyone.* New York: Scholastic, 1997.
———. *Chicken, Chicken, Don't Go to Sleep.* New York: Scholastic, 1997.

Look carefully at each book and answer the following questions.

- What makes the book stand out from others on the shelf?
- Does the artwork and cover design invite you to pick up the book and have a look?
- If you didn't already know that the book wasn't produced

by an "official" publishing house, could you tell the difference?
- What approach do you think the book packager could have used to sell the idea to a publisher?
- Can you find mention of the book packager on the title or copyright page? (Don't be surprised if you can't. Some publishers like to keep their relationship with packagers a trade secret.)

IS THERE A BOOK INSIDE YOU?

There's only one way to find out if there are any good book ideas inside you, and that's to take a good look. Dan Poynter's book *Is There a Book Inside You? A Step by Step Plan for Writing Your Book* (Santa Barbara, Calif.: Para Publishing, 1995) might help you find out. Read it, follow the plan as far as you can, and see if you still like the idea of writing and producing books.

WHO'S WHO IN PUBLISHING?

A book packager can have a million great ideas, but unless he or she can match an idea with the right publisher, it won't become a book. That's why book packagers have to do their homework and learn who's doing what in the publishing industry. Here are three ways to start learning the business yourself.

1. Go to a bookstore or library, find books that appeal to you, and look at the copyright page to see who published it. Find the address of the company and write to request a catalog of their entire list of books.
2. Go to the reference section of the library, find *Literary Marketplace* (a new edition is published each year by R.R. Bowker), look up the names of publishers that you have heard of, and see what kinds of books they list as examples of recent publishing efforts.
3. Go to a big book festival and visit different publisher's exhibit booths. You can find out about events like this in the book section of your community's Sunday newspaper.

CHECK IT OUT

American Book Producers Association
160 Fifth Avenue, Suite 625
New York, New York 10010

National Association of Independent Publications
P.O. Box 430
Highland City, Florida 33846

Small Press Writers and Artists
13 Southwood Drive
Woodland, California 95695

GET ACQUAINTED

Susan Lingo, Book Packager

CAREER PATH

CHILDHOOD ASPIRATION: To be a storm-chaser tracking down tornadoes.

FIRST JOB: Worked as a clerk in a health food store.

CURRENT JOB: Author, publisher, and owner of Bright Ideas Books.

A STRANGE THING HAPPENED ON THE WAY TO THE CLASSROOM

Susan Lingo actually started her professional career as a teacher. In fact, she has taught every grade except fifth grade. Several years ago, when her family moved to a new state, Lingo couldn't find a teaching position. She decided the time was right to follow the advice of some of her fellow teachers and write a book about her ideas for making learning fun.

Lingo had so many ideas that she thought the best approach might be to write a magazine for teachers. That way she could introduce new ideas every month. She put together a proposal and sent it to a publisher. The publisher rejected the magazine concept but liked her ideas so much that she was asked to do 14 books instead. Obviously, Lingo's career as an author was launched in a big way. Today, Lingo has 42 books (and counting) to her credit.

ONE THING LEADS TO ANOTHER

Writing all those books put Lingo in contact with lots of publishing houses. They began to know and respect her work. One publisher liked her work so much that she offered Lingo a job as the editor of her children's book division. Lingo accepted the position on the condition that she could keep on writing her own books.

As it turns out, the experience (like most big experiences in life) had its pros and cons. On the good side was the opportunity to learn the fine points of publishing and be part of the process from beginning to end. For Lingo, the down side of the job was the editing. Instead of working in the creative realm of her own ideas, she ended up fixing other people's mistakes. She found the role of manuscript mender to be very frustrating and eventually decided to stick with what she does best—writing her own books.

MOVING ON DOWN THE ROAD

This time Lingo decided to blend her writing experience with her publishing experience and actually produce her books for publishers. This way she retains complete creative control of the project from beginning to end and can make it happen the way she sees fit. Lingo still writes the manuscripts and comes up with the overall concept of how the book should look. Then she hires designers and editors to do the rest.

As Lingo continues to crank out books, she's found the following six steps to be key to her success as a book packager.

1. Recognize a need for a book and respond to that need with a good idea.
2. Write an outline that is complete enough that someone else can understand what the book would be about.
3. Prepare a proposal and sample chapters.
4. Match the book idea with a publishing house that does similar books.
5. Make the pitch and close the deal.
6. Deliver such a great product that publishers come back for more.

BEYOND ONCE UPON A TIME

Lingo echoes the sentiment that book packagers should "go with what they know." She says it would have been impossible for her to write and produce the learning activity books that she focuses on if it hadn't been for her classroom experience as a teacher.

She says that if you want to produce books, you need to start with books that you find interesting. Lingo also says that the most important skill you'll need to develop as a writer is self-discipline. The books won't write themselves!

Bookseller

SKILL SET

- ✔ BUSINESS
- ✔ TALKING
- ✔ WRITING

SHORTCUTS

GO compare one of the book superstore chains with a privately owned bookstore.

READ *American Bookseller*, the magazine of choice for book merchants. Find a copy at your local library or request one from *American Bookseller*, 828 South Broadway, Tarrytown, New York 10591.

TRY volunteering at your school's book fair (or talk to the school librarian about hosting one).

WHAT IS A BOOKSELLER?

First, a clarification: There really isn't a particular career called bookseller. Instead, there are several different ways to make a living selling books. Such careers are explained in the following pages.

Bookstore owners enjoy the dream job of many a book lover. Running their own business, surrounded by good books and other literary fans, is the perfect combination for a fun job. At its best it can be fun, stimulating, and profitable. Competition from the gigantic bookstore chains, however, has made it more challenging for independent bookstore owners. Those who succeed tend to do so by carving out a unique niche. Whether it's with mysteries, children's books, audio books, educational materials, or CD-ROM products, small bookstores can offer what the big guys can't in terms of specialized service and expertise and, quite often, in a fun environment to indulge one's fancy for a particular genre.

Bookstore managers keep things running smoothly in larger bookstores and bookstore chains. They do this in much the same way that any business manager would, by handling administrative tasks such as hiring and scheduling staff, keeping track of inventory, and providing customer service.

Book buyers are the people who decide which of the thousands of new books published each year get space on the bookstore shelves. Buyers may work for the corporate headquarters of one of the major chains, a larger independent bookstore, a school district, or a university. Their job is to keep the shelves stocked with books readers will want to buy. Buyers must stay current with what's hot and new in publishing by meeting with publisher's representatives, attending trade shows, and reading lots of catalogs and industry publications. The tricky part is making educated guesses about how well each book will sell, being prepared for overnight sensations (as a guest appearance on a television talk show might spark), and staying one step ahead of the latest trends and fads. Look at the sale table in any bookstore to find evidence of bad calls by book buyers and overzealous publishers.

Publisher's representatives are employed by a specific publishing house or work independently for any number of companies. Their job is to introduce books to book buyers. A representative is generally responsible for a specific and sometimes sizable region, called a territory, so they often spend a good deal of time traveling around to the places where books are sold—bookstores, school districts, universities, and trade shows. Equal parts of salesmanship and marketing savvy are required to do this job well.

Many of these career ideas lend themselves to on-the-job learning opportunities or even official apprenticeships. Working in a bookstore is a good first step toward any of these options. Higher level positions such as book buyer may require training or experience in business or marketing as well. In addition, some publishers look for expertise in a specific area. This is especially true for working with educational or academic books where many reps are experienced teachers.

For someone who loves good writing and has an interest in business, a career in book sales can be a great choice.

TRY IT OUT

BOOK EXCHANGE

You don't have to be grown up and have lots of money to run your own bookstore. All you need are a few friends who like to read and are willing to trade some books from their own collections. To participate, ask everybody to bring a couple of books to share. Give each person a certain amount of credit for every book that they bring. You might designate the credit with index cards, bookmarks, or even play money from a board game. You'll want to make rules about things such as whether a hardcover book is worth more than a paperback and so forth.

Arrange a special time and place for everyone to get together and use their credit to "buy" books. For a special touch (and extra fun), you might want to serve refreshments, play some music, or otherwise set the tone for a lively literary experience.

ON-LINE WINDOW SHOPPING

Thanks to the Internet, you no longer have to live in a big city to have access to the best bookstores. Go on-line to visit bookstores all over the world at http://www.bookwire.com. Along with links to many bookstores, this site also contains a wealth of information about the book industry. You'll find tips and tools for bookstore owners, news updates, and a calendar of events, as well as some fascinating statistics about books.

The American Booksellers Association hosts another website you'll want to visit. You can find it at http://www.ambook.org/. It contains all kinds of insider information that any book lover would find fascinating.

THE TOP SELLERS

Find a current list of best-selling books. Your library, a bookstore, or the book section of the Sunday newspaper will list them. Or go on-line to look at the *New York Times Book Review* at http://www.nytimes.com.

Pick a book and follow its progress for a couple weeks to see how it does. Also, whenever possible or appropriate, read some of the best-sellers to see what all the fuss is about. As you read, try to imagine why that particular book made it to the top. What makes it so special?

AND THE WINNER IS . . .

There are the best-sellers, and there are the award-winners. Sometimes you'll find the same books on both lists, but sometimes you won't. Remember, best-seller doesn't necessarily mean the best read. Find out about the awards and the winners at http://www.bookwire.com/index/book-awards.html. Some of the most prestigious awards include the Pulitzer Prize, the Nobel Prize for literature, the National Book Award, and the Coretta Scott King Award. For children's books, the Caldecott and Newbery medals are among the most respected and coveted. Make sure to add some of the best book titles to your summer reading list!

CHECK IT OUT

American Booksellers Association
828 South Broadway
Tarrytown, New York 10591-5112

Information Industry Association
559 New Jersey Avenue, Suite 800
Washington, D.C. 20001

National Association of Publishers Representatives
295 Fifth Avenue, Suite 621
New York, New York 10016

GET ACQUAINTED

Clara Villarosa, Bookstore Owner

CAREER PATH

CHILDHOOD ASPIRATION: To be a teacher.

FIRST JOB: Working for a seamstress.

CURRENT JOB: Owner of the Hue-Man Experience, the largest African-American bookstore in the United States.

A NEW DIRECTION

Clara Villarosa had always wanted to be a teacher and started college with that goal in mind. After a while, she discovered that there was more to the education field than teaching. She changed her college major and went on to earn a master's degree in social work. She began her career as a psychiatric social worker in a mental health clinic.

FULL-TIME MOM

While her children were young, Villarosa worked outside the home one day a week and spent the rest of her time being a full-time mother. When her youngest child entered school, Villarosa worked part-time. Then the family moved from Chicago to Denver, and Villarosa went to work at Children's Hospital as chief psychiatric social worker in the department of behavioral sciences. After working at the hospital for a number of years, she advanced to assistant hospital administrator.

BACK TO SCHOOL

When Villarosa's children were in college, she decided to join the party and went back to school too. She started working toward a doctorate degree (a Ph.D.) in social work. As happens to a lot of students, she ran out of money before she finished the program. Oh well! On to the next stage of her life!

INTO THE BUSINESS WORLD

The next stop on Villarosa's career journey took her to a major bank. Her management skills led her all the way up to a position as assistant vice president of human resources and strategic planning. Meanwhile, though, she had this idea in the back of her mind: She wanted to own her own bookstore. So while she was working at the bank, Villarosa started saving money. Eventually she'd saved enough, along with the help of two partners, to open a very small version of her dream bookstore. The store continued to succeed over the years and has now become the largest African-American bookstore in the country.

The store specializes in African-American and African books with sections of fiction, history, children's, and religious books. It has a large selection of magazines, greeting cards, unique gifts, and fine art prints.

THE COMMUNITY CONNECTION

Owning your own business requires more than good business and management skills. Villarosa says it is important to have a close connection with the community where you do business. She says this is particularly important for anyone running an ethnic business.

IT'S NOT ALWAYS EASY

It's not easy running your own business. A person must be creative and be a self-starter who can handle lots of different roles. There isn't a boss to make you do the job, and sometimes there aren't even other workers to share the load. Especially when you are just getting started, you are it, and if you don't do it, it won't get done. Villarosa says if you have a vision, it takes hard work and focused energy to start and run a business.

KEYS TO SUCCESS

Villarosa believes it is critical for young people to have a love of reading. So much of education is based on reading. She says to start reading early and develop a real appreciation for books and learning. Two other skills important in any walk of life are speaking skills and writing skills. She puts it very simply: read, write, and speak well.

Corporate Communicator

SKILL SET

- ✔ BUSINESS
- ✔ TALKING
- ✔ WRITING

SHORTCUTS

GO to the library and ask to see some of the annual reports submitted by local businesses.

READ the business section of the newspaper and look for quotes by company spokespeople.

TRY visiting the website of a favorite company.

WHAT IS A CORPORATE COMMUNICATOR?

Getting the word out about a company in a way that builds a positive image is the main function of a corporate communicator. Corporate communicators use their top-notch verbal and written communication skills to convey carefully crafted messages about the company they represent. To do so, the job may include working with the media and other sources to reach an external audience (that is, all the people who are touched by the company, from the neighbors who live near the place of business to its paying customers). Likewise, corporate communicators also need to effectively stay in touch with internal audiences (the company's employees). This is especially important in large corporations that may employ thousands of people in dozens of locations.

Some of the tools that corporate communicators use to reach these audiences include press releases, newsletters, brochures, annual reports, multimedia presentations, and bulletin board displays. Technology has added some new tools to the list in the form of some fairly sophisticated telephone or computer e-mail information systems. It is estimated that businesses spend a combined total of around $1 billion on internal communication activities alone, so you can imagine that there is plenty of work to do in this profession.

Corporate communicators go by many job titles including public relations specialist, corporate communications director, community affairs coordinator, communications specialist, press secretary, public information officer, and spokesperson. Corporate communicators often specialize in a particular area within the company. Specialties within the profession include

community relations, which involves developing activities that allow a business to give something back to the community where the business operates. This area might include special events, volunteer programs, and charitable giving projects.

government relations, which involves monitoring and influencing legislation that affects the company.

investor relations, which involves keeping investors informed about the company and its financial status. Preparing annual reports and coordinating shareholder meetings are part of the job.

corporate training, which involves providing in-house workshops and training sessions about topics such as communication skills, diversity, and gender equity.

A college degree is essential for corporate communicators. Majors in areas such as communications, public relations, business, or marketing are good educational choices for those interested in this line of work. Fluency in a foreign language is considered a plus in today's global economy.

There are three ways to boost your chances for landing a good job in this field. One way is to get involved in community volunteer programs. Another is to take advantage of every work-study, cooperative education, or internship opportunity that comes your way in order to gain some real work experience. The third is to spend time working or living in another culture, perhaps as an exchange student or Peace Corp volunteer. Surround yourself with people who speak another language, and your communication skills are guaranteed to improve!

TRY IT OUT

WHAT IF

Corporate communicators have to be prepared for anything. In fact, these professionals are often asked to prepare step-by-step plans for handling potential crises, such as an earthquake or an injury resulting from the use of the company's products. These plans provide scripts and action plans so that everyone knows exactly what to do in case, heaven forbid, something bad happens.

Pretend that you are the person in charge of handling public relations for your school. Here are a couple scenarios for you to consider. Make a plan to come through these mini-disasters with as little trouble as possible. Each plan should have at least five steps.

- A bus breaks down on the way to school during a snowstorm.
- The cafeteria runs out of food before everyone is served.
- Half of the teachers don't show up for school one day.

THE SPIN DOCTOR IS IN

Corporate communicators must learn quickly how to make the most of a bad situation. Their job is to put a positive spin on a bad situation; however their job is *not* to lie or deceive. Honesty is the name of this game. Only a fool would try to get away with lying to the public.

Suppose your school has decided to add an extra hour to the end of every school day. The principal is concerned that the students and staff might not receive this news very well. She asks you to come up with a plan for presenting the news in a way that will make the idea more agreeable to everyone.

What would you do? First, come up with some good reasons and then develop promotional materials such as posters and special events that might help soften the news.

THE INTERNET MARKETPLACE

It probably won't surprise you that Internet websites are becoming a very popular means for businesses to communicate with their audiences. Take a look at some of these popular sites and see how they do it:

http://www.adidas.com
http://www.levi.com
http://www.nike.com
http://www.revlon.com
http://www.sony.com

CHECK IT OUT

American Society of Hospital Marketing and Public Relations
840 North Lake Shore Drive
Chicago, Illinois 60611

Association of Business Communication
University of North Texas
College of Business
Department of Management
Denton, Texas 76203

International Association of Business Communicators
1 Hallidie Plaza, Suite 600
San Francisco, California 94102

Public Relations Society of America
33 Irving Place
New York, New York 10003

Women in Communications
2101 Wilson Boulevard, Suite 417
Arlington, Virginia 22201

GET ACQUAINTED

Chris Chavez, Corporate Communicator

CAREER PATH

CHILDHOOD ASPIRATION: To be a pro-football quarterback.

FIRST JOB: Washing pizza pans at Godfather's Pizza.

CURRENT JOB: Community relations manager at AT&T–Western Region.

OUT OF THE QUESTION

Chris Chavez really wanted to be a pro-football quarterback, but when he stopped growing at the not-so-menacing height of 5'8", he decided he should probably pursue another career. He grew up in Laramie, Wyoming, where his mother was a Spanish teacher and his father, a conductor for the Union Pacific railroad. He attended schools in Laramie and excelled academically in high school. College was the logical next step.

A PROUD MOMENT

Chavez is very proud of the fact that he is the first male member on either his mother's or his father's side of the family to go to college. He was accepted at both Stanford University and Notre Dame, but the necessary financial support was not available for him to attend. He received a full scholarship to the University of Wyoming, where he majored in journalism.

EENY, MEENY, MINEY, MO

After graduation, Chavez was offered two jobs. One was a position as assistant press secretary for then-Congressman Dick Cheney (Wyoming). The other job offer came from Jackson Hole, Wyoming. The job was outdoors editor for the *Jackson Hole Guide* (which at that time was the top weekly newspaper in the country).

Chavez took the job in Jackson Hole. He needed a break after four hard years of college. Through his job he was able to enjoy and simultaneously write about downhill skiing, fly fishing, kayaking, canoeing on the Snake River, and climbing the Teton Mountains. He won five state awards for news, feature, and column writing. He worked at the paper for two and a half years.

GIVE THE CORPORATE WORLD A TRY

Next Chavez decided to try his hand at corporate public relations. He was hired by the Martin-Marietta Astronautics Group (the company that designs components for the space program). He went to work as public relations manager. He was thrilled to be working for a major corporation, making a good salary, and able to spend money on himself. Unfortunately, he was laid off nine months later when government contracts were cut. It was time to look for another job, so he hit the streets again.

A COMMUNITY FOCUS

Chavez was fortunate to land a job as public relations director for Downtown Denver Partnership, a private, nonprofit promotional agency for downtown Denver, Colorado. He says it was a wonderful job. During his years there, Chavez promoted notable events such as the pope's visit to Colorado, and the opening of Coors Baseball Field, a new downtown library, and an amusement park. Downtown Denver was coming into its own, and Chavez was right in the middle of it. He worked with the media and wrote speeches, brochures, and annual reports.

CORPORATE WORK WITH A COMMUNITY TWIST

After five years, Chavez started thinking about a career change and moving on to other challenges. He was going through some other life changes as well, including getting married. When Chavez returned from his honeymoon, he received a call from an executive recruiter asking him if he was interested in a new job. One month later, he was hired by AT&T. He is now in charge of the company's community relations for 14 states.

Chavez handles community outreach and events, works with the media, is the liaison and representative in the western section of the country for the AT&T Foundation, and administers Foundation funds. He also handles employee volunteer programs and spends a lot of time reviewing proposals from groups wanting money for various programs.

SOME PROFESSIONAL ADVICE

Chavez believes that one of the most important things for a young person to do is to identify a mentor or a role model—someone you look up to and want to be like. Talk to them or write to them; ask them how they got where they are. It's important to have someone to identify with and to ask for advice.

GOOD WRITERS ARE GOOD READERS

If you want to go into the writing field, it is critical that you be a good reader. Chavez advises reading at least one book a month and one or two newspapers a day. Keep up on current events, study how people write, and most importantly, do your own writing.

Keep a journal (keep it private if you don't want anyone to read it), and practice sentence structure. Be creative, and keep your mind open to what's going on in the world! There are always opportunities for those who look hard enough.

Editor

SKILL SET

- ✔ COMPUTERS
- ✔ TALKING
- ✔ WRITING

SHORTCUTS

GO tour a large print shop to find out how books are produced.

READ a favorite magazine and look at the masthead, which lists many of the people it took to put the issue together. You'll discover that publishing is a team effort!

TRY helping your English teacher edit student essays. See how many grammatical errors you can find and fix.

WHAT IS AN EDITOR?

Editors make sure that the books, magazines, newspapers, and other publications that you read provide correct information and are written clearly and grammatically. A good word to describe an editor's role in the publishing process is *liaison,* or go-between. In one sense, an editor is the liaison between a book's author and its readers. The job here is to do everything possible to assure the best quality of work for the reader's enjoyment. The editor works with an author throughout the writing process to help shape a writer's ideas into content suitable for publication.

In another sense, an editor acts as liaison for the publisher, acquiring new books and negotiating contracts that are mutually beneficial for the authors and the publisher. This part of the process can be as mundane as digging through the "slush piles," or stacks of unsolicited manuscripts, that are found in every editor's office—although this is where editors sometimes find the perfect new book to add to the publisher's list—to as glamorous as having lunch with a best-selling author to discuss ideas for his or her next book.

Another way that editors act as liaison is with the production staff. In production, manuscripts become books, and the process involves artists, page designers, and printers. An editor must maintain a clear vision of the "identity" of each book in order to guide the creative team in producing a look that is suitable.

Finally, the editor typically serves as go-between with the marketing department. It won't matter how well the book is written and how nicely it's designed if there isn't a solid plan for getting the book into the hands of readers. It all comes down to selling books, and the editor is often one of the best resources for helping this process move in the right direction.

In short, editors have to be good jugglers because they are responsible for many aspects of the publishing process. It's a lot to do for one book, but imagine what's it like to be responsible for dozens of books in various stages of development. It can be demanding but very exciting work.

Fortunately, in many publishing houses, the various tasks of an editor are shared by more than one person. In fact, in larger houses, there are specific types of editors who are responsible for specific parts of the editorial process. Following are descriptions of the different types of editors.

Editorial assistants handle the nitty-gritty details of the editorial office in a manner similar to a clerk or secretary. However, due to the nature of their work and proximity to more experienced professionals, they are often being primed for bigger and better things within the publishing house.

Assistant editors help sort through the sometimes massive slush piles, screening manuscripts, responding to queries from authors, and assisting in other ways.

Associate editors assume similar duties as assistant editors but have more responsibility for managing projects from beginning to end.

Editors handle many of the same aspects of a project as associate editors, but full-fledged editors tend to work on more important books. In addition to working with authors and agents to acquire books from submitted manuscripts, editors may also come up with their own project ideas and manage all the processes of turning the ideas into books.

Senior editors manage other editors and work on major projects. Senior editors also handle more of the administrative aspects of the process such as long-range plans, budgets, and sales projections. In smaller publishing companies, the senior editor assumes much of the responsibility for acquiring new books as well.

Acquisitions editors are constantly on the lookout for good books to add to their publisher's list. They read many manuscript submissions and proposals, conduct research on the book's marketability, and select projects that will enhance their list. Knowing the audience and understanding what it wants to read are crucial elements for the success of an acquisitions editor.

Copy editors are among the last people to read a manuscript or other publication before it goes to print. They correct the facts, continuity, grammar, sentence structure, and spelling, and they make sure that everything is absolutely perfect before the manuscript goes to print.

Publishers tend to hire editors with college degrees in areas such as liberal arts, English, and communications. Even with a college degree, most editors start at the bottom of the editorial career ladder as editorial assistants. However, with hard work, talent, and initiative, an editor might expect to start moving up that ladder rather quickly.

TRY IT OUT

GET YOUR ACT TOGETHER

Organization is key to any editor's success. Get used to the idea of using your time wisely by making a schedule and keeping it. First, either buy a daily planner or make your own time chart. Go easy on yourself and start with a schedule for just one day. Include all the tasks you'd normally do such as eat and sleep and list the day's classes as "appointments." Make sure to allow time for after-school activities and a detailed plan for completing your homework assignments. Pretty soon keeping your act together will become habit.

Next, move on to the bigger picture. Use space in your daily planner or devise another time chart to make a long-term plan. This might involve a big project that you have to do for a class, or it could involve a plan for something like training for a big athletic competition, completing a big paper for a class, or earning money to buy a new bike (or even a car). Whatever your goal is, you'll need to designate a start and finish time. Leave space in between to list all the things you'll have to do in order to reach your goal. Give each step a date and specific instructions. As new things come up, add them to the plan and keep moving forward toward reaching your goals.

GIVE YOUR TEXTBOOK A MAKEOVER

Go to your locker and pull out your least favorite textbook. Thumb through the textbook, and make a list of the things you don't like about it. The fact that it's a math book and you hate math isn't exactly what you are after; rather, think about those elements that make it hard or unpleasant to read.

After you've identified its bad points, make a list of the elements that you like. Perhaps the use of color livens things up or the sidebars, maps, or tables that are included with each chapter are easy to understand.

Finally, pretend that you are the editor at a textbook publishing house and have been asked to update this textbook for a new edition. Write a letter to your publisher describing the ways you think the book could be improved to better meet the needs of its intended audience. Perhaps include a sample revised page or a photocopy of a page on which you have edited and updated.

THE CYBEREDITOR

Computers play a big part in the editorial process. Editors use them for things such as keeping track of projects, researching new ideas, communicating with authors, and editing manuscripts. Following are a few editorial hangouts on the Internet:

- Editor and Publisher Interactive at http://www.mediainfo.com provides links to nearly 2,500 Web-based newspapers and easy access to research, the latest news, special events, and other resources.
- Editorial Eye at http://www.eeicom.com/eye/ provides interesting articles about editing.
- Copy Editor at http://www.copyeditor.com provides updates on language usage and style, as well as answers to sticky copyediting questions.

READ WHAT EDITORS READ

The following resources will keep you current on what's happening in the publishing industry and introduce you to some of the people and publishers that might become your future employers. Find copies in your local library, write for a free sample issue, and check out their very informative websites.

Folio: The Magazine for Magazine Management
Cowles Business Media
911 Hope Street
P.O. Box 4949
Stamford, Connecticut 06907-0949
http://www.folio.com

Publishers Weekly
249 West 17th Street
New York, New York 10011
http://www.publishersweekly.com

CHECK IT OUT

American Society of Magazine Editors
575 Lexington Avenue
New York, New York 10022

American Society of Newspaper Editors
P.O. Box 4090
Reston, Virginia 22090

Association of American Publishers
71 Fifth Avenue
New York, New York 10003

Editorial Freelancers Association
71 West 23rd Street, Suite 1504
New York, New York 10014

Freelance Editorial Association
P.O. Box 380335
Cambridge, Massachusetts 02238

National Conference of Editorial Writers
6223 Executive Boulevard
Rockville, Maryland 20852

Society of American Business Editors and Writers
University of Missouri School of Journalism
76 Jannett Hall
Columbia, Missouri 65211

GET ACQUAINTED

Eileen O'Reilly, On-Line Editor

CAREER PATH

CHILDHOOD ASPIRATION: To be a reporter or talk show host.

FIRST JOB: Scooping ice cream at Baskin-Robbins.

CURRENT JOB: Senior producer for the on-line website Student Center.

A MULTIMEDIA CAREER

During the course of Eileen O'Reilly's career, she has had the opportunity to work with words in several different types of media. O'Reilly majored in political science at the University of Colorado at Boulder; after graduation, she headed east to New York City, America's "media center."

She got her start working in production for *House and Garden* magazine. Since this magazine happens to be published by one of the biggest names in the business, Condé Nast, O'Reilly found plenty of opportunity to move up the ranks in this company. She eventually made her way to a senior editorial position after learning the ropes at magazines such as *Glamour, Vanity Fair, Traveler,* and *Self.*

After working several years on magazines, O'Reilly decided to change mediums, turning to television shows. Working on various projects for PBS (the Public Broadcasting System) and local affiliates, she discovered a whole new dimension in editing. Instead of working primarily with words and pictures at a desk, this job took her all over the city researching and filming segments.

Next stop on the career path was a job with a publisher of interactive CD-ROM products. Once again, O'Reilly found herself faced with the challenge of learning a completely new way of communicating information. Putting together the content for a project focusing on American Sign Language involved incredible organization skills and attention to details. The pace was completely different from her work in television, as she found that just one project could consume more than a year of intense effort.

O'Reilly's most recent challenge has been working for a fairly new start-up company that specializes in developing on-line products.

A NEW FRONTIER

As producer of the Student Center, a career and job search website that helps students find out about different careers, research specific companies, and prepare résumés for their first venture out into the workplace, O'Reilly is amazed at the constant flow of information. Not only does she and the entire Student Center team keep a steady flow of new information moving into the website, but the users constantly provide instant feedback and interactive communication via the chat rooms and user polls that are part of the site. It's a completely different experience from working in magazines where everything is done with three months lead time. It's especially exciting to O'Reilly because it's a whole new means of communication, and she's there at the very beginning to help figure out how to make the most of it.

A TURNING POINT

O'Reilly says that it was a college internship that got her interested in a career in communications. She worked for a public relations firm and had the chance to be involved in projects involving famous sports figures, a fashion magazine, and sports events. It was here that she discovered what having a real job was really like. She learned how to dress for an office job, arrive on time for work, and work as part of a creative team.

THE PEOPLE MAKE THE DIFFERENCE

One of the best parts of working in the media is the people. O'Reilly says that she especially enjoys working with the bright, interesting people she's found everywhere in this profession.

In addition, O'Reilly has found that networking with others in the profession has been the key to some of the really exciting opportunities that have come her way. Quite often, meeting someone who knows someone else who was doing something interesting led to O'Reilly's new jobs. She's also had the opportunity to learn from watching others succeed in the business. One of the perks of her current job is helping the women who founded the company forge new ground in this exciting new field of communication.

SEE FOR YOURSELF

O'Reilly invites you to join some of the 9 million or so monthly visitors to her website and see what you think of her work. You can find it at http://www.StudentCenter.com. Although the site is geared toward students who are in high school or college, you'll find some great information about preparing yourself for the real world of work.

Freelance Writer

SKILL SET

- ✔ ADVENTURE
- ✔ BUSINESS
- ✔ WRITING

SHORTCUTS

GO visit the place where your local newspaper is published.

READ *The Elements of Style* by William Strunk Jr. and E. B. White (New York: Macmillan, 1978). It's a classic that makes learning the basics of grammar interesting.

TRY writing an article for your school newspaper.

WHAT IS A FREELANCE WRITER?

Freelance writers are writers for hire. They aren't actually employed by a specific company; instead, they work on various projects from a variety of sources. In a sense, they run their own businesses with their writing skills being the product offered for sale.

Freelance writers find that potential clients are everywhere. Virtually every magazine found on supermarket shelves is filled with submissions from freelance writers. Newspapers often run feature stories written by freelance writers. Textbooks, encyclopedias, and other reference books are commonly filled with the work of freelance writers. In addition, some publishers hire writers to work on books for a specific project under development.

Two other lucrative areas for freelancers are business writing and technical writing. Businesses of all kinds and sizes often hire freelance writers to work on projects such as proposals, speeches, annual reports, newsletters, brochures, and other publications. Some freelance writers work exclusively for public relations firms; advertising agencies, in particular, will use experienced writers to help with various projects. This way the agency handles the marketing aspects of finding clients, and the writer focuses on pleasing the client with well-crafted written materials.

Technical writers are currently in big demand to translate software programs and other complicated documents into instructions that just about anyone can understand. Technical writing isn't for everyone. Sometimes the work requires a writer to have very specialized technical knowledge as well as top-notch writing skills.

Although the pay isn't always quite as good, some freelance writers specialize in working with nonprofit organizations and charities. The ability to write clear and convincing grant proposals is a hot commodity among agencies that depend on funds from foundations and benevolent corporations for their support.

Instead of receiving a salary like an employee or royalties like an author, freelancers are generally paid a flat fee. There is a big gap between low-end and top-end fees: Some projects pay as little as a few cents per word, while others pay a generous hourly rate and still others, on a per-project basis.

Just like other independent business people, freelance writers must spend a good portion of their time marketing their services. This generally involves plenty of research, lots of good ideas, and many letters. The most successful freelancers take a very businesslike approach to their writing and are careful to market their services in a very professional manner. They don't wait for business to come to them. Instead they are constantly seeking out writing assignments from a variety of interesting sources.

It is quite common for freelance writers to start out writing part-time in addition to holding down another job. They continue to moonlight as writers until they've built up the experience and clientele to maintain a steady income from their writing.

More than anything else, it's a freelance writer's way with words that keeps the writing assignments coming. Writing well is the only credential that counts; however, education and experience can be the keys to opportunities for freelance writers to prove their skills. Most people who succeed as freelancers have a college background in fields such as liberal arts, communications, or journalism and have gained experience working as a journalist, public relations writer, or editor. Writers with an entrepreneurial sense of adventure and deep reserves of creative ideas may find their future in freelance writing.

TRY IT OUT

READ TO WRITE

There are a number of helpful resources you can read to learn how to be a good writer. Some you'll want to investigate include

---

Otfinoski, Steve. *Putting It in Writing.* New York: Scholastic, 1993.

Seuling, Barbara. *To Be a Writer. A Guide for Young People Who Want to Write and Publish.* New York: Twenty-First Century Books, 1997.

Willett, Lou. *Thinking Like a Writer.* New York: Random House, 1994.

Other books provide a good overview of what it's like to earn a living as a freelance writer. To get the inside scoop on this profession, try

Cassill, Kay. *The Complete Handbook for Freelance Writers.* Cincinnati: Writer's Digest Books, 1980.
Meredith, Scott. *Writing to Sell.* Cincinnati: Writer's Digest Press, 1995.
Oberline, Loriann Hoff. *Writing for Money.* Cincinnati: Writer's Digest Press, 1994.

Another source of information about opportunities for writers is the *Writer's Digest* magazine. Pick up a current issue at your local bookstore or request information about subscribing from *Writer's Digest* magazine, Writer's Digest Books, 1507 Dana Avenue, Cincinnati, Ohio 45207.

WRITING IN CYBERSPACE

Some Internet websites you won't want to miss include the following:

- Children's Writing Resource Center at http://www.write4kids.com is for people who want to write books for children or young adults. It offers lots of tips for beginners and links to some fun (and free) stuff to download.
- Inkspot at http://www.inkspot.com is a comprehensive site for professional writers featuring articles, interviews, market information, research tips, and a guide to the best Internet resources for writers. There's also a special spot just for young writers at http://www.inkspot.com/young/.
- OWL (On-Line Writing Lab hosted by Purdue University) at http://owl.english.purdue.edu boasts more than 130 instructional handouts about writing that you can consult. Here you can also gain access to on-line help with your school writing assignments.
- Writer's Workshop at http://www.english.uiuc.edu/cws/wworkshop/ww_hand.html provides links to nearly 100 websites where you can find advice on the writing process.

WORDS FOR SALE

Freelance writers have to know where to find clients and how to please them. Two tools make it easier to accomplish this. Go to the reference section of your local library and find the *Literary Marketplace* (New Providence, N.J.: R.R. Bowker, 1998) and *Writer's Market* (Cincinnati: Writer's Digest Books, 1998). With these two rather bulky books, you'll have located thousands of potential clients. Take some time to thumb through and learn a little bit about some of them.

GET A HEAD START

Who says you have to be an adult to be a freelance writer? If you've got the skills (and the courage), there are plenty of places to get your work published starting now. The following resources include information about outlets for young writers as well as contests, camps, and other resources.

Dils, Tracy E. *Young Author's Guide to Publishers.* Cincinnati: Raspberry Publications, 1996.

Henderson, Kathy. *The Market Guide for Young Writers: Where and How to Sell What You Write.* Cincinnati: Writer's Digest Press, 1995.

Rising Voices: A Guide to Young Writers' Resources. 2nd ed. New York: Poets and Writers, Inc., 1997.

CHECK IT OUT

American Medical Writers Association
9650 Rockville Pike
Bethesda, Maryland 20814

American Society of Journalists and Authors
1501 Broadway, Suite 302
New York, New York 10036

Associated Business Writers of America
1450 South Havana Street, Suite 620
Aurora, Colorado 80012

Education Writers Association
1331 H Street NW, Suite 307
Washington, D.C. 20005

National Writers' Association
1450 South Havana, Suite 424
Aurora, Colorado 80012

Writers Alliance (East)
555 West 57th Street
New York, New York 10019

Writers Alliance (West)
8955 Beverly Boulevard
West Hollywood, California 90048

GET ACQUAINTED

Naomi Wax, Freelance Writer

CAREER PATH

CHILDHOOD ASPIRATION: To be a poet or writer.

FIRST JOB: Playground duty for a parks and recreation program.

CURRENT JOB: Freelance writer and editor.

BEATING THE SYSTEM

Naomi Wax is unusual in that she has been a freelance writer and editor from day one of her professional career. She says that probably 99 percent of freelance writers start out working in-house for a magazine or book publisher, get some experience, make some contacts, and then go out on their own. Of course, she didn't know that at the time. Sometimes ignorance is bliss!

Wax graduated from the University of Michigan with a degree in English. The first year out of school was spent in Israel traveling around. She returned to live in New York City and got a job working as a waitress until she could figure out what she really wanted to do with her life. She knew she wanted to work in publishing, but she also knew that she didn't want to start at the bottom and spend a couple years typing and filing as an editorial assistant. She had nothing to lose, so she put together a résumé and sent letters offering editing and proofreading services to several book packagers. This wasn't the standard approach for breaking into the publishing industry, but it worked.

A LUCKY BREAK

Wax says the turning point for her career came when she met the head of the research department at *Condé Nast Traveler*, a travel magazine. It just so happened that the magazine was getting ready to publish several articles on Israel and needed someone who knew something about country to verify some details. Since Wax had just spent a year there, she was hired as a fact checker.

This project got her foot in the door and helped her make contacts that launched her career as a freelance writer and editor. Wax now realizes that it was a smart move to start out in the research department. Research work allowed her to work closely with the articles and with a variety of editors. She learned a lot about so many different things and made great contacts with people who continue to be sources of work and encouragement.

ALL IN A DAY'S WORK

Wax loves the freedom and the variety that come with being a freelance writer. Being self-employed, she is free to choose her own hours and the types of projects she works on. Since she loves to travel, it is not unusual for her to work day and night for a few months and then take off for a few weeks to some intriguing part of the world such as Turkey, Ecuador, or Peru.

Working on a wide variety of projects keeps things fun. For instance, recent assignments have included writing biographical sketches about women writers, an in-depth magazine article about estate tax law, and a short piece on her experience in Turkey for a travel magazine. Another project was doing a major overhaul on an Internet website for a travel magazine.

Depending on the project, Wax may work from home or onsite at a client's office. A project may last for a few days or for a few months. She accepts a variety of projects that involve writing, editing, research, training, or a combination of these skills. She's found that having the option to mix and match her skills helps prevent burnout and keeps her ready to tackle the next challenge—whatever that may be!

A LITTLE OF THIS, A LITTLE OF THAT

Wax does quite a bit of work for magazines and has had articles published in magazines such as *Condé Nast Traveler, Vanity Fair, Mirabella,* and *Elle.* Her articles tend to focus on beauty, finance, or travel. In fact, Wax is working on perfecting the art of the working vacation. Whenever she has the itch to go somewhere, she pitches story ideas. That way every vacation is an almost all-expenses-paid vacation (there are still a few kinks in the plan)!

Wax has also written articles for various books. Two examples are *Cool Women: The Reference* (Los Angeles: Girl Press, 1998) and the *Encyclopedia of New York City* (New Haven, Conn: Yale University Press, 1995). Look for these books in the library and see what can happen when someone with a lot of talent and initiative creates a job for him or herself.

Grant Writer

SKILL SET

- ✔ BUSINESS
- ✔ TALKING
- ✔ WRITING

SHORTCUTS

GO do some extra chores and donate your earnings to a nonprofit organization whose work you admire.

READ about some prominent nonprofit organizations such as the American Red Cross, the American Humane Society, or the Public Broadcasting System.

TRY writing a proposal to your parent(s) asking for a raise in your allowance.

WHAT IS A GRANT WRITER?

Grant writers are expert at asking for money. They approach carefully selected corporations, foundations, the government, and wealthy individuals to request money for nonprofit organizations or charities. The catch is that the giver gets nothing in return except the knowledge that he or she has used money to do something good (and get a few tax breaks); therefore, soliciting grant money works best when the grant writer asks someone to support programs that fit with the interests of that individual. For instance, a grant writer for a university might ask a former graduate (who also happens to be a multimillionaire) to help fund a new science facility. This simple strategy changes the dynamics of the process from begging for money to matching money with opportunities to make a difference.

Grant writers must use words to paint compelling pictures of the projects that need funding. Since they are generally dealing with busy people with little time wading through well-intentioned junk mail, they must be able to describe complex projects in concise, well-defined terms. Quite simply, they must make it as easy as possible for a donor to say yes and write a check.

Although writing is a big part of the job, it's only one part of it. Before a grant writer sits down to write a proposal, he or she has to do lots of homework. A grant writer must know just about everything about the nonprofit organization represented in the proposal. An extra dose of persuasive passion is added to the process when the writer really believes in the work being done by the organization.

Another of a grant writer's homework assignments is finding out as much as possible about the people and organizations being asked for money. Fortunately, many groups with an interest in charitable giving publish reports and other documents that provide helpful background information. Grant writers look for additional information at the library and in the newspaper to understand fully the organization's interests and giving patterns.

Quite often grant writers find that it is not enough to just know about someone or some organization. It also helps to get personally acquainted with the people behind the checkbooks. Networking and building relationships with funders is often part of a grant writer's job.

Grant writers are generally employed in the development department of nonprofit organizations. In a small organization, a grant writer may be the entire development department. In larger companies, a development director, or development officer, may head a whole team. And, instead of actually employing grant writers, some organizations may hire freelance writers to prepare grant proposals.

As with many writing careers, there isn't a direct path into grant writing. Some grant writers have experience in other kinds of writing, while others have a background in public affairs or nonprofit administration. Quite often, grant writers land in their positions by discovering a perfect fit for their writing skills in helping further a cause that is important to them.

Although there isn't a particular college degree associated with grant writing, many grant writers find it well worth the time and effort to take courses in grant writing. These courses are offered by various colleges and professional associations and can help you learn the ropes of this very specialized type of writing. Grant writing can be a good choice for a writer who likes people and wants to use his or her talent to make the world a better place. There's nothing quite like a writer with a cause.

TRY IT OUT

JOIN THE CLUB

Nonprofit organizations everywhere would welcome your interest in volunteering. Even though you don't get paid, carefully chosen volunteer projects will give you two important benefits. First, you get a chance to lend a hand to a cause you believe in or enjoy. Second, it gives you experience and contacts for future reference.

Be prepared: Most volunteering involves varying degrees of behind-the-scenes drudge work. Play it smart, and give every task your best effort. These things have a way of paying big dividends down the road.

ON-LINE HELPERS

The Internet is where you can find out about all your favorite funders. Pick any major corporation, use a web browser to find their website, and find out how (and if) they give back to their communities.

While you're on-line take a look at some of these useful sites.

- The Grantmanship Center at http://www.tgci.com. Here you'll find grant-writing tips and leads on good sources of funds. You'll also find links to other sources of interest to professional grant writers and fund-raisers.
- Gain access to Internet Resources for Non-Profit Public Service Organizations via http://www.lib.va.edu/smr/pr3.htm. This site will take you to all kinds of nonprofit organizations, corporations, and government programs. It's just the spot for all that background research!
- Society for Nonprofit Organizations at http://danenet.wicip.org/snpo. More tips, more statistics, and more links to other useful resources is what you'll find at this site.

LEND A HAND

If your school is like most schools, you'll find plenty of opportunities to ask people for money. Whether it's selling candy bars for the sports team or finding advertising sponsors for the yearbook, there are plenty of ways to start learning how to ask for money.

The next time your school has a fund-raiser, get involved. Do all you can to make it a success. While you are at it, keep your eyes and ears open, and notice what kinds of projects work the best. Talk to people who sell the most, and find out the secrets to their success. It might even be useful to put together a little report to share your findings with the teachers or coaches in charge of the project.

THE NONPROFIT ROAD TO RICHES

Grant writers can learn a lot from other grant writers. For one account of a very enterprising approach to fund-raising, read *Filthy Rich and Other Nonprofit Fantasies: Changing the Way Nonprofits Do Business in the 90's* by Richard Steckel (Berkeley, Calif.: Ten Speed Press, 1989).

CHECK IT OUT

Foundation Center
79 Fifth Avenue, Eighth Floor
New York, New York 10003

Independent Sector
1828 L Street NW
Washington, D.C. 20036

National Academy on Volunteerism
701 North Fairfax Street
Alexandria, Virginia 22314-2045

National Society of Fund Raising Executives
1101 King Street, Suite 700
Alexandria, Virginia 22314
800-666-FUND

Nonprofit Management Association
1309 L Street NW
Washington, D.C. 20005

GET ACQUAINTED

Elizabeth Curtler, Grant Writer

CAREER PATH

CHILDHOOD ASPIRATION: To work for the State Department in other countries or to be a newspaper reporter.

FIRST JOB: A summer secretary for the U.S. Department of Education.

CURRENT JOB: Director of corporate and foundation relations at George Washington University.

FIRST IMPRESSIONS ARE LASTING IMPRESSIONS

Elizabeth Curtler believes that a person's first work experience can play an important part in establishing the direction that his or her career takes. For instance, one summer when she was in college, she worked for a government agency that was responsible for awarding fellowships to students pursuing higher learning experiences. This work experience, along with her jobs as an English teacher and a community college administrator, gave her a place to put her words to work. She's been writing to help various academic institutions raise funds for a number of years now.

EVERY DAY IS A LEARNING EXPERIENCE

Working as Curtler does in a university provides a fascinating opportunity to learn about a wide variety of subjects. Curtler has been involved in writing proposals for projects that involve subjects as diverse as automobile safety, chemistry animation, Korean studies, and contemporary art. Although there are times that she claims to know about as much about a given subject as you could hold in a very small thimble, she takes every opportunity to ask questions about what each project involves and why it is important.

EVERY WORD COUNTS

When Curtler approaches a foundation or corporation, she is often asking for millions of dollars to fund very important work. With that much at stake, it's worth taking the time to learn as much as she can about each project. It's also extremely important that Curtler use good judgment in matching the right funders with the right projects. That takes lots of homework, but it pays off when those big checks show up in the mailbox.

A LAST RESORT

Curtler says that writing is hard work. So hard, in fact, that she doesn't sit down at her computer to write a grant proposal until she's sure the time is right. Two things tell her it's time to get writing. First, everyone involved in the project knows what to say. That means that the ideas about the proposed project have been hammered out enough so that its purpose is clear and easily defined. Second, the people Curtler's approaching for funds are ready to hear what the proposal has to say. Reaching this stage of the process involves using two types of skills—verbal communication skills and people skills. Curtler must invest time and energy in developing relationships with people before asking them for money. It's one of her favorite parts of the job.

THANK GOODNESS FOR DEADLINES

Even after writing professionally for a number of years, Curtler sometimes finds herself at a loss for words. She says it can be a challenge to get started on a new project. Fortunately, she works under a lot of deadlines, so sometimes she has no choice but to sit down and just write. Curtler calls this being backed in a corner by a deadline.

One thing that helps her get going is knowing that the first thing she writes is never final. There's always the opportunity to go back and make it better.

A FEW WORDS FOR FUTURE WRITERS

The more you read, the better you write, says Curtler. She urges those with an itch to write to read all kinds of new things. Everything you read gives you new ideas about words and the way they are used.

As for learning to become a writer, Curtler believes that doing it—writing—is the only way to learn it. One way to get practice is to share your writing talent with people and organizations who might need it—your church or synagogue, a volunteer organization, or even a family member. Writing is something you can do to help others.

Information Broker

SKILL SET

- ✔ ADVENTURE
- ✔ COMPUTERS
- ✔ WRITING

SHORTCUTS

GO to the library and browse through the books in the reference section.

READ *The Information Broker's Handbook* by Sue Rugge and Alfred Glossbrenner (New York: McGraw Hill, 1995).

TRY picking a subject of interest and seeing how much information you can dig up about it.

WHAT IS AN INFORMATION BROKER?

Information brokers are part researcher, part writer, and part investigator. Often hired to find the most obscure and elusive types of information, information brokers must exhaust every resource on the trail of the answer. Chasing down elusive information often sends information brokers cruising down the information highway.

In fact, computers and other technology were the catalysts that started this whole profession in the first place. The Internet, CD-ROM databases, and other sources of information opened a whole world of resources for skilled information brokers to glean from. These resources put at one's fingertips information that might otherwise take days, weeks, or even longer of painstaking research (and sometimes extensive travel) to find.

The information is out there. However, as anyone who has tried to find specific information on the Internet can attest, it takes skill and resourcefulness to navigate the system in search of what you need. In addition to all the high-tech methods, an information broker is also no stranger to libraries, news files, government record agencies, and other sources of hard-to-find information.

Information brokers are sometimes employed by corporations but are just as likely to be self-employed. Self-employed information brokers can work from a home office or from a business suite. Clients from anywhere in the world can be served professionally thanks to the convenience and affordability of technology such as computers, faxes, and modems, and the efficiency of overnight mail. Who needs to know that the information broker is sitting at the kitchen table working in pajamas?

An information broker may serve a variety of different types of clients—anything from a start-up business to a major Fortune 500 conglomerate. Some specialize in a particular area such as medical research, legal issues, or other technical research. Advertising agencies and public relations firms are frequent users of information brokers, as are publishing houses and educational institutions.

A profession closely related to that of information broker is that of researcher. Publishers of magazines, reference books, and other types of nonfiction books often have a research staff who use their skills in two ways. One way is to verify the facts found in complex articles or soon-to-be published books. The other way is to collect new information for projects that are in progress. The latter is

called primary research and is usually the domain of more experienced researchers.

Working on the research side of publishing can be a great way to learn about a particular subject or about publishing in general. Since researchers often have to rewrite incorrect data or compile reports detailing their findings, it also provides an opportunity to gain valuable writing skills.

As for training requirements, there are none officially. If you've got the equipment, the skills, and the clients, you are in business. There's a catch, of course. The skills and the clients are likely to be more readily available with training and experience on your résumé. Some of the most successful information brokers and researchers have a background in library science, which allowed them to master some of the finer arts of in-depth research.

TRY IT OUT

THE INFORMATION BROKER TEST, PART 1

You think you'd like to be an information broker or researcher, do you? Take this little test to see if you've got the right stuff.

Go to the reference section of a well-stocked library and see how long it takes to find the answers to the following questions.

- In what year did Grover Cleveland begin his second term as president of the United States and what was unusual about it?
- What was the birthplace of author Mark Twain (aka Samuel Clemens)?
- What was the batting average of baseball great Babe Ruth?

By the way, feel free to ask for help if you need it. Any good information broker knows when it's time to call in reinforcements.

THE INFORMATION BROKER TEST, PART 2

Back for more, are you? This time return to the reference section of the library with notebook and pencil in hand. Find the following reference books and jot down a few notes about the types of information you find in each one.

- *Books in Print* (New Providence, N.J.: R.R. Bowker, 1998).
- *Encyclopedia of Associations* (Detroit, Mich.: Gale Research, 1998).
- *World Almanac and Book of Facts, 1998* (Mahwah, N.J.: Funk & Wagnalls, 1997).

SHAKE THE FAMILY TREE

Tracing your family's history can provide an interesting and informative introduction to the research process. Start by asking questions. Ask parents, grandparents, and other relatives for details about other branches of the family tree. Record everything you discover and how you discovered it. You may also find useful information in the genealogy section of a major library.

If you find yourself hooked on this process, you may want to invest in some inexpensive computer software. One excellent resource is the Family Tree Maker by Broderbund. It's available in both standard and deluxe versions and includes nine CDs full of helpful resources such as birth and marriage certificates, census data, and Social Security death records. Look for this software at your local computer or office supply store or contact the publisher directly for information. Broderbund's toll-free phone number is 800-521-6263.

CRUISING FOR ANSWERS

Take advantage of all the wonderful resources available on the Internet. Start looking, and you'll find more information than you'll know what to do with. If you have access to America Online, click into their Research and Learning channel for access to all sorts of encyclopedias, dictionaries, and other reference materials. Another good place to start your search is the Research It! website. This site can be found at http://www.itools.com/research-it/research-it.html. Here you can look up words in a variety of dictionaries, be able to translate words from one language to another, find equations, and lots more.

CHECK IT OUT

Information Industry Association
1625 Massachusetts Avenue NW, Suite 700
Washington, D.C. 20036

Information Professionals Institute
46 Hiller Drive
Oakland, California 94618

GET ACQUAINTED

Sue Rugge, Information Broker

CAREER PATH

CHILDHOOD ASPIRATION: To find a job—any kind of job.

FIRST JOB: Worked in camera shop owned by her father.

CURRENT JOB: Coprincipal of the Information Professionals Institute, coauthor of *The Information Broker's Handbook,* and owner and operator of Italia Reservations.

AN EARLY START

Sue Rugge's career began out of necessity. She married at an early age and became the mother of two sons. She hadn't gone to college and didn't have many marketable skills at the time, but the young family needed her help to keep food on the table. She found a job as a night circulation clerk in a library where she checked books in and out and "stamped a lot of cards."

TRAGEDY STRIKES

Rugge's husband was killed in a car accident, leaving her a widow at the age of 21 with two young sons to support. Rugge went to work as a typist for General Motors Defense Research Laboratories and was assigned to the company library. There, she typed catalog cards and interlibrary loan slips.

For the next few years, she worked in several different corporate libraries. Typically, it was her typing skills that got her the job, but she spent the time learning everything she could about research. The last company that Rugge worked for went bankrupt, and she found herself out of work.

KNOCKING ON DOORS

Rugge was not the only person without a job. California was in economic doldrums and many people (more educated than Rugge) were looking for jobs. Rugge decided she did not want to go back to the typing pool. She started knocking on corporate doors. She thought if she could find five companies that would hire her to do research one day a week, that would be a pretty good job. No one took her up on her offer. What to do?

Then Rugge met a librarian who liked the idea of doing research on a project basis. Together they founded a company called Information Unlimited. They made their services available to those with whom they had networked, many of them founders of the computer industry in Silicon Valley. Eventually, people started to call asking for copies of articles, patents, etc. That was the beginning of their information brokering business. They found a need and filled it!

WHAT EXACTLY DO YOU DO?

Essentially Rugge and her partner had created a new profession. No one had heard of "information brokers," so Rugge had lots of explaining to do: An information broker gathers information from a variety of sources to satisfy their clients; a fee is charged for providing the information; information itself is not sold. Their expertise in knowing how to obtain the needed information in the most thorough and cost-effective manner became their selling point. They used databases of all kinds, on-line databases, the Internet, print resources, and the telephone to supply their client with reliable and comprehensive information in a useful format.

BREAKING UP IS HARD TO DO

After the original business partnership broke up, Rugge founded her own company—Information on Demand. She built the company into a leader in the information field, with annual sales of $2 million. That company was eventually sold, and Rugge continued to work for the new owner for three more years.

Tired of working for someone else, Rugge decided to start yet another company, something a little different this time.

R&R FOR B&BS

Rugge set about contacting bed and breakfast inn (B&B) owners and convincing them that they needed an occasional break for rest and relaxation (R&R). She would run the inn while the owners went on vacation. Thus, her company, Innkeepers Respite, was born. She did this for several years until she got tired of being away from her own home so much that she decided to go back to her original occupation.

WHEN THE WORST HAPPENS

The Rugge Group, a coalition of independent information professionals, offering research in a variety of fields, was formed. Everything was going smoothly until a fire struck. Rugge's home, possessions, and business (which was operated from home) were lost. All the information was gone. It was a nightmare come true.

This didn't stop Rugge. Somewhere along the way, Rugge had learned to pick herself up and keep on going. She rebuilt the business and eventually sold it when the itch for doing something new hit again.

ANOTHER NEW START

Still interested in the business, Rugge and two other information industry entrepreneurs founded the Information Professionals Institute (IPI). She is now coprincipal of the institute. IPI conducts seminars (both general and custom-designed) across the country for those wanting to learn how to access the best information possible from the best sources. The institute also serves as a resource center for aspiring and experienced information professionals. Rugge also coauthored *The Information Broker's Handbook*, which is now in its third edition.

THE NEXT CHAPTER

Rugge is now moving into another phase. She has set up a website with annotated bibliographies of books useful to aspiring researchers and brokers (you can visit her site at http://www.ipn.net/ipi). She will also continue to sell the book she coauthored. She is, however, leaving a good portion of her information research business behind as she embarks on yet another career.

Rugge's new company, Italia Reservations, provides weekly and monthly rentals of property in the Tuscany area of Italy. This gives her an opportunity to travel and do what she loves best—marketing.

Journalist

SKILL SET

- ✔ ADVENTURE
- ✔ TALKING
- ✔ WRITING

SHORTCUTS

GO visit the offices of a newspaper and get a sense of the fast-paced, no-nonsense side of journalism.

READ national and local newspapers and magazines to see how journalists write about the news.

TRY writing a story about an event at your school for the community newspaper.

WHAT IS A JOURNALIST?

Who won the 1997 World Series? What's going on in the Middle East? Should you wear a coat to school tomorrow? If you know the answers to these questions, chances are that it is because of the work of a journalist. Journalists, or reporters, are the people who write stories about the people, places, and events that shape our world. The latest news about sports and fashion, as well as developments in Third World countries and outer space, are brought to our doorstep and television sets compliments of journalists who meticulously track down the facts and report them in news stories.

Writing late-breaking news is quite a bit different from other kinds of writing. Articles must be factual, informative, free from the reporter's bias, and concise. Reporters must continually find new ways to build stories around the six key elements of a journalistic report: who, what, where, when, why, and how.

Successful journalists must develop a nose for news and be able to make quick decisions about whether a particular event is news or not. They often must wrestle with ethical dilemmas such as when the public's right to information overrides a person's right to privacy.

Probably the most consistent challenge facing any journalist is the time-crunch issue. Stories of even the utmost importance must be investigated and written quickly and accurately. Competition between various news sources makes this even more of a rush as everyone wants to "scoop," or be first with, a new story. Once a newspaper hits the streets, there is no way to take it back, so journalists have to get the story right the first time.

The work of a given journalist might be as routine as covering a local school board meeting or as heartbreaking as covering the aftermath of a terrible tragedy. Some journalists, particularly those reporting from war zones or in other volatile situations, work under life-threatening circumstances.

Journalists are typically assigned a "beat" and work on specific types of stories such as local news, sports, or education. No matter what beat they are assigned, effective journalists share two traits. One trait is curiosity. Journalists have to be full of questions. The second trait is persistence. Journalists must have the energy and drive to do what it takes to find the answers.

If you'd like to become a journalist, plan

on earning a college degree in journalism, communications, English, or political science. Also, plan on starting at the bottom of the ladder in the newsroom. The most exciting stories tend to go to the more experienced journalists. Make sure to take advantage of every opportunity to get experience by working on school newspapers and actively seeking internship opportunities while you complete your education.

Perhaps the best perk of the job is that thousands and even millions of people might read a journalist's work each day. This is a privilege that few other writing professions enjoy. Journalists get the opportunity to have a major impact on their world. Wars, environmental debates, and many a political career have been won or lost via the power of the press.

TRY IT OUT

FOLLOW THAT STORY!

Look in the first section of a major newspaper and find a major story. It might be about a natural disaster, a political issue, or an international event. Cut out the headline story and any associated stories, sidebars, or charts. Continue to follow the story until its resolution. Keep track of significant details and take note of how the story is reintroduced to readers on subsequent days. Make sure to note which page the story appears on each day as this will provide important clues to the story's continued importance in the scheme of world news. You'll also want to keep track of the reporters! Is it the same person everyday? Does it vary?

If possible, follow the story from more than one source. Take notes about coverage on various television and radio stations. Read and clip stories about the same event that appear in other newspapers. Check the Internet or your library's microfiche files for related coverage. Compare the stories and how they are covered. Notice what elements are emphasized in each story. Can you identify the reporter's angle? Can you detect any bias in the report?

GO AFTER THE NEWS

It goes without saying that if you want to be a journalist, you should work on the school newspaper or yearbook. Both of these outlets can provide invaluable first experiences in scooping out news events, covering them, and writing stories to inform. Keep copies of your best work to include in your professional portfolio.

READ ALL ABOUT IT!

Following are some interesting books for you to read about journalists and their work.

Blaney, Retta. *Journalism: Stories from the Real World.* Golden, Colo.: North American Press, 1995.

Harrigan, Jane T. *Read All About It! A Day in the Life of a Metropolitan Newspaper.* Chester, Conn.: Globe Pequot Press, 1988.

Ricchiardi, Sherry, and Virginia Young. *Women on Deadline: A Collection of America's Best.* Ames, Iowa: Iowa State University Press, 1991.

SATURDAY NIGHT AT THE NEWSROOM

Your local video store is the place to find some interesting fictional portrayals of journalists. Ask your parents if you can rent movies such as *All the President's Men, The Absence of Malice, The Paper,* and *Broadcast News.* All provide fairly accurate portrayals of life in the newsroom.

INSTANT NEWS

We've got fast food, so why not fast news? The Internet is the source of news as it happens, when it happens. Find out how journalists keep the world informed on the information highway by visiting some of these hot news spots.

http://www.cnn.com
http://www.foxnews.com
http://www.usatoday.com

CHECK IT OUT

American Society of
Journalists and Authors
1501 Broadway, Suite 302
New York, New York 10036

American Society of
Newspaper Editors
11690B Sunrise Valley Drive
Reston, Virginia
20191-1409

Dow Jones Newspaper Fund
P.O. Box 300
Princeton, New Jersey
08543

National Newspaper
Foundation
1627 K Street NW, Suite 400
Washington, D.C. 20006

Newspaper Association of
America
Newspaper Center
11600 Sunrise Valley Drive
Reston, Virginia 22091

Newspaper Guild
8611 Second Avenue
Silver Spring, Maryland
20910

Newspaper Publishers
Foundation
1401 Wilson Boulevard,
Suite 207
Arlington, Virginia 22209

Society of Professional
Journalists
P.O. Box 77
Greencastle, Indiana 46135

GET ACQUAINTED

Debbie Becker, Journalist

Becker and friend at the 1998 Winter Olympics in Japan.

CAREER PATH

CHILDHOOD ASPIRATION: To be a forest ranger.

FIRST JOB: Worked as a gofer for the *Washington Post.*

CURRENT JOB: Sports reporter for *USA Today.*

THE RIGHT PLACE AT THE RIGHT TIME

Along with a talent for writing and knowledge of a number of sports, Debbie Becker also has a knack for being in the right place at the right time. She landed a job with the *Washington Post* by joking with a friend to put in a good word for her with his editor. He did, and she got a job.

The same holds true with her present job. *USA Today* was just a new, upstart newspaper when Becker graduated from college, and they immediately hired her. Today the paper is read by some 2 million readers every weekday.

A WOMAN IN A MAN'S WORLD

As a freshman lacrosse player at the American University in Washington, D.C., Becker was disappointed to find out that the school paper covered only men's sports events. When she went to the office to complain, she found out that the only reason women's sports weren't covered was because there was no one to write the stories. Becker volunteered to start reporting on these neglected events, discovered she liked it, and a career was born.

Sports is still a male-dominated world, and Becker often finds herself as the only woman in the press box at many events. To get where she is today, Becker has had to work extra hard and watch her step, but she wouldn't trade the experience for anything.

OLYMPIC-SIZED BEAT

Becker has reported on the Winter Olympics in Calgary, the Summer Olympics in Barcelona, and the Summer Olympics in Atlanta. She specializes in covering gymnastic, figure skating, and cycling events. This beat involves more than just covering the main Olympic games. Long before the world gathers to compete, there are trials and national championships to keep track of. Becker particularly likes doing stories on unknown athletes in minor sports and on women athletes because it gives her a chance to recognize people who've worked hard and are often overlooked.

THIS JOB HAS PERKS

Olympics, World Series, Super Bowl—Becker has been there, done that, seen it. As a journalist, Becker gets to see lots of events for free—the same events that others pay top-dollar for, if they can get tickets at all.

ADVICE TO FUTURE SPORTS JOURNALISTS

Get all the internship experience you can so that you can find out what you like and what you're good at. Becker had originally planned to get into television broadcasting, but an internship experience taught her that she didn't like it at all, so she refocused her attention on newspapers.

Librarian

SKILL SET

- ✔ COMPUTERS
- ✔ WRITING
- ✔ TALKING

SHORTCUTS

GO visit every library you can find—school, public, corporate, law, etc.

READ *Booklist* or *American Library*, two magazines published by the American Library Association. Find the latest issues at your local library or request a sample copy from American Library Association, 50 East Huron Street, Chicago, Illinois 60611.

TRY creating a mini-library with your own book collection.

WHAT IS A LIBRARIAN?

Keeping rowdy readers in line is just one small part of a librarian's job. According to the American Library Association, librarians are professionals who organize and preserve recordable information and knowledge, provide library and information services, and deliver information products.

On first guess, you might think of a librarian (sometimes called a multimedia specialist) as the person who helps you find information for research papers and check out books. If so, you are only partially correct. This type of librarian works in an area called user services, which involves dealing directly with the public (the users of a library). Places where you might find this type of librarian at work include the reference section of the library, the circulation desk, and the children's department.

Another type of library work is technical services. These librarians work behind the scenes acquiring new books and materials, cataloging books for the library's database, and otherwise preparing and protecting the materials that are placed on the library shelves.

The third area of library work is in administration. Much like any other business or government agency, someone must handle the day-to-day operations that keep a library running smoothly. Administrative duties may include managing the people who work in a library, ordering equipment and supplies, planning and keeping track of budgets and expenses, raising funds to support the library, and handling public relations. It is an especially good choice for someone who has an interest in the business side of the library.

In addition to these three main types of library work, there are increasing opportunities for blending expertise in computer technology with a library career. In the past, most libraries kept track of their collections with card catalogs. New computer automated information retrieval systems make the process much easier and efficient. Professionals with the skills needed to plan and operate these highly specialized computer systems are in big demand.

Librarians of all types can be found in several different kinds of libraries. You may already be familiar with the public library and your school library or multimedia center. Other places where librarians work are in academic libraries at colleges and universities and special libraries that serve organizations such as businesses, government agencies, museums, law firms, and medical centers. Special libraries offer librarians an opportunity to blend a personal interest such as art or medicine with their general interest in books.

To become a full-fledged librarian, you'll need a master's degree in library science from a program accredited by the American Library Association. You can earn your undergraduate degree in almost any area, although some would say that a well-rounded liberal arts education might be an ideal choice. In the meantime, while you are earning your degrees, there are many opportunities to work in a library as assistants and technicians.

New technology and the information highway continue to pave the way for exciting new opportunities for librarians as information managers. If working with books, people, information, and technology sounds like a winning combination for your future, read on.

TRY IT OUT

JUST THE FACTS, PLEASE

Books aren't the only thing you find at libraries these days. For many people, the library provides their first and sometime only access to the Internet. That's why librarians have to stay one step ahead of the rest of the crowd on the information highway. One way that they do this is by using a number of Internet resources.

Where the Wild Things Are, an award-winning website, proclaims itself to be a librarian's guide to the best information on the Net. It includes everything from a general reference desk and quick access to medical expertise to professional resources that deal with topics such as discouraging plagiarism and understanding copyright laws. The site is fun and easy to use. You can find it at http://www.sau.edu/CWIS/Internet/Wild/Index.htm.

Librarian Web Resources is the place to go to find all kinds of other sites related to libraries. From here you can reach professional associations, national libraries, vendors, and other useful information sources. Find it at http://www.scsu-cs.ctstateu.edu/library/libtools.html.

For a dose of library humor, visit Alex the Librarian. This online comic strip can be found at http://tln.lib.mi.us/~krentzin/alex.htm. For a free Alex sticker send a self-addressed stamped envelope to Alex the Librarian, 4157 Cooper Street, Royal Oak, Michigan 48073.

A LIBRARY OF OPPORTUNITY

Make a list of all the different kinds of jobs you might find in a library or in information services. Several were mentioned in this section. Look for other ideas in books such as the following:

Heim, Kathleen, and Peggy Sullivan. *Opportunities in Library and Information Science.* Lincolnwood, Ill.: VGM Career Books, 1984.

Mount, Ellis. *Opening New Doors: Alternative Careers for Librarians.* Washington, D.C.: Special Libraries Association, 1993.

Rugge, Sue, and Alfred Glossbrenner. *The Information Broker's Handbook.* New York: McGraw Hill, 1995.

Sellen, Betty-Carol. *What Else You Can Do With a Library Degree: Career Options for the '90s and Beyond.* New York: Neal-Schuman Publishing, 1997.

Mark off three columns in the space next to your list. Use the first column to indicate whether each job deals mostly with people, books, or technology. In the second column, jot down a few details about what each job involves. In the last column, make note of any special skills or knowledge requirements (for example, medical background for a hospital library, or art history for an art museum).

The last step is to use a highlighter or colored marker to indicate which of the jobs sound most interesting to you. Now, it's up to you to find out all you can about the best route for a library career that blends all your interests and talents.

TEACH SOMEONE TO READ

It seems fairly logical that if you are interested in libraries, you're probably a pretty big fan of books as well. If that's true for you, you've already discovered what a great treasure it is to be able to read.

There are many people, however, of your own age as well as older and younger people, who do not know how to read. Fortunately, you can help.

Ask your local librarian about literacy organizations in your area or contact the American Literacy Council, 680 Fort Washington Avenue, New York, New York 10040, or the Barbara Bush Foundation for Family Literacy, 1002 Wisconsin Avenue NW, Washington, D.C. 20007.

Once you've gotten in touch with a group near you, volunteer to help someone learn to read. Many literacy groups will provide training to help you get started. But, if all else fails, find someone who doesn't know how to read and just start reading to them.

LEND SOME TIME TO A LIBRARY

The best place to find out if library work is a good career choice for you is at a library. Talk to your school or public librarian about your interest, and volunteer to help out. You'll probably start out by reshelving books. Okay, so it can get a bit tedious, but it's a great way to learn the Dewey decimal system. Once you get going, look for other ways to help out. The children's summer reading program may be a good place to experience more of what it's like to work in a library.

Other places where you might put your newly found library skills to good use are at a church or synagogue, a health care facility for the elderly, child care centers, and neighborhood associations. Volunteering can be a fun way to prepare for your future while making life a bit brighter for others.

CHECK IT OUT

American Association of
Law Libraries
53 West Jackson Boulevard,
Suite 940
Chicago, Illinois 60604

American Library Association
50 East Huron Street
Chicago, Illinois 60611

American Society for
Information Science
8720 Georgia Avenue, Suite 501
Silver Spring, Maryland 20910

Art Libraries Society of
North America
4101 Lake Boone Trail, Suite 201
Raleigh, North Carolina 27606

Association of Research
Libraries
21 DuPont Circle, Suite 800
Washington, D.C. 20036

Medical Library Association
6 North Michigan Avenue,
Suite 300
Chicago, Illinois 60602

Society of American Archivists
600 South Federal, Suite 504
Chicago, Illinois 60605

Special Libraries Association
1700 18th Street NW
Washington, D.C. 20009-2508

GET ACQUAINTED

Wayne Crocker, Library Director

CAREER PATH

CHILDHOOD ASPIRATION: To be a football player.

FIRST JOB: Delivering newspapers and mowing lawns.

CURRENT JOB: Director of the Petersburg Public Library system in Virginia.

PLAN B

Like a lot of young boys, Wayne Crocker had high hopes of a career as a professional football player. All the way through school he'd played football, baseball, and basketball, and he was pretty good. When he got to high school and it came time to try out for varsity basketball, he was competing against the likes of classmate Moses Malone for a spot on the team. When Crocker didn't make the team, he realized that there might be a little more to school than playing sports. He was surprised to discover how much there was to learn and applied himself to learning all he could.

Looking back now as a grown-up, he can say that not making the team was a good thing. It helped him focus his efforts in other areas and start thinking about what to do with his life.

THE START OF A BRAND-NEW LIFE

Crocker had always been a hard worker. He started delivering newspapers when he was just 11 years old and kept busy cutting lawns for several years (he even took care of the grass at a local cemetery). One of his friends worked at the Petersburg (Virginia) Public Library and told him that they had an opening for another library page. He had not used the library very much up to that point, but working in a cool, quiet place sounded like a nice change of pace from cutting grass in the hot sun, so he applied for the job and got it. Little did he know that this opportunity would shape his entire life.

ONE GOOD TURN AFTER ANOTHER

Crocker continued working at the library all the way through college. Along the way he'd been promoted to library aide and continued to enjoy the work. During his senior year in college, the library director took him aside and encouraged him to apply for a scholarship to receive a master's degree in library science.

As a business major, Crocker had been entertaining thoughts of working for a Fortune 500 company after he graduated. But the library director was not someone who took no for an answer, so Crocker went ahead and applied for the scholarship. That's how he won a full scholarship to earn a master's in library science degree from Atlanta University.

BACK TO WHERE IT ALL BEGAN

While working on his master's degree, Crocker got a job at the Atlanta Public Library. There he worked on a retrospective conversion process in which all the books and materials in the library system were converted to a machine-readable format. It was a big job, but he worked hard and found that it all paid off when he was offered a job as a librarian in the system. Atlanta was just finishing a new state-of-the-art library, so it was a really exciting place to work.

Crocker was happily minding his own business in the job, when the same Petersburg library director who'd convinced him to apply for a scholarship decided to retire. She encouraged Crocker to apply for her job. A little reluctant at first, Crocker put in an application. The former library page got the job and went back home as director of three libraries (the main library and two branches). It was a dream come true.

HOME, SWEET HOME

The fact that Petersburg is home to Crocker makes it especially satisfying to be in such an influential position. It motivates him to get involved and make a difference in the community. His community involvement takes many forms. He's active as a mentor to young people, and he participates in a number of community boards and commissions. He also serves as Petersburg's legislative liaison and keeps track of legislative issues that affect the community.

IF LIBRARIES ARE IN YOUR FUTURE

Libraries aren't just four walls and books anymore. Crocker is excited about the way that computers and other technologies are turning libraries into information and communication centers. Pretty soon the library will be the place to go for contact with an entire world of information. Crocker sees an exciting future for young people who know how to learn, think, and focus.

Literary Agent

SKILL SET

- ✔ BUSINESS
- ✔ TALKING
- ✔ WRITING

SHORTCUTS

GO scrutinize several books in the children's section of the library. Choose which books you'd have been most proud to represent as a literary agent.

READ *Publishers Weekly* for an introduction into what's happening in the publishing industry. Find copies at your local library or contact *Publishers Weekly*, 249 West 17th Street, New York, New York 10011 (but a subscription is rather expensive).

TRY practicing your negotiating skills the next time your friends have a disagreement.

WHAT IS A LITERARY AGENT?

Literary agents are one of the links between writers and publishers. They represent authors in getting manuscripts and book proposals to editors who can publish them. To accomplish this, literary agents must wear several hats. First, they must be book critics. Out of all the manuscripts that cross their desks, literary agents must be able to pick the winners. This requires a broad yet discerning interest in books of all kinds and an understanding of what publishers look for in books. Literary agents cannot skimp on this step if they expect to be in business for long. Publishers need to be able to trust the literary judgment of the agents they work with. They count on agents to weed out the junk and send books with the potential to make it big. A literary agent must be very careful to guard his or her reputation as a reliable source of good books.

Second, literary agents must be editors. In fact many successful literary agents actually get their start in the business as editors. Wearing the editorial hat, literary agents must be able to recognize the raw potential of a manuscript, spotting those "diamonds in the rough" and guiding a writer through the process of polishing it up. Recognizing that the book may only get one shot at being picked up by a publisher, the agent wants to get the manuscript in good shape.

The third hat that literary agents wear is that of matchmaker. Literary agents have to match the right book with the right publisher. They have to know the special interests of each publisher and make connections with key decision-makers in the business. Literary agents who know how to "work the crowd" and meet editors and publishers at conventions, trade shows, and other publishing events have an edge over those who simply submit manuscripts with a polite cover letter attached.

Business manager is another hat worn by literary agents. Once an agent carefully selects a promising project, fine-tunes the manuscript, and finds a good publisher, it is time to close the sale. Authors depend on their agents to negotiate the best possible terms for their work. This part of the process can get rather complicated when issues such as royalties, copyright, foreign rights, and (for the ever-hopeful fiction writers) movie rights enter the picture. Some literary agents have a legal background or seek legal counsel for this part of the process.

Since literary agents work on commission and get paid only when a book is sold, they are very picky about the authors they choose to represent. In addition to representing writers, some agents work with songwriters and playwrights as well. Literary agents may work in an established agency or start their own.

Most literary agents find that training and experience in the publishing industry is essential to their success. A college background in journalism, English, communications, marketing, or even law can provide effective training for this profession.

TRY IT OUT

THE INSIDE STORY

Literary agents have to know what it takes to pick a winner and push it to the top of the book business. You can get a jump start on the process by reading books such as the following:

Curtis, Richard. *Beyond the Bestseller: A Literary Agent Takes You Inside the Book Business.* New York: New American Library, 1989.

Jenkins, Jerrold R., with Mardi Link. *Inside the Best Sellers.* Traverse City, Mich.: Rhodes and Easton, 1997.

THE INSIDE TRACK

The Internet provides some exciting resources for and about literary agents. Following are descriptions of a couple you won't want to miss.

- http://www.simonsays.com/kidzone is where you'll find all kinds of interesting information about authors and illustrators.
- http://www.authorlink.com is a news, information, and marketing source for editors, literary agents, and writers.
- http://www.inkspot.com/market/agents.html includes information specifically for literary agents as well as links to directories of practicing agents.

READ 'EM AND WEEP

Most major newspapers include literary reviews in their Sunday editions. Here book critics express their sometimes brutally honest opinions about books of various genres (categories such as mystery, self-help, etc.). Read through the review section of your local newspaper or go on-line to read what the critics at the *New York Times* have to say at http//www.nytimes.com.

BE A SKEPTIC

What makes a book a best-seller? By what merit does a book win a national award? Read a couple of best-sellers and/or award-winners to find out. Assume the role of a book critic, and decide for yourself what makes it so hot. You may find that you disagree with the "experts." That's fine, as long as you have some good reasons to back up your decision.

CHECK IT OUT

Association of Talent Agents
9255 Sunset Boulevard, Suite 318
Los Angeles, California 90069

Society of Authors' Representatives
10 Astor Place, Third Floor
New York, New York 10003

GET ACQUAINTED

David Hendin, Literary Agent

CAREER PATH

CHILDHOOD ASPIRATION: To be a doctor or a baseball player.

FIRST JOB: Performed magic shows from age nine through college.

CURRENT JOB: Literary agent.

FROM TEACHER TO JOURNALIST

David Hendin grew up in St. Louis. After he graduated from college, Hendin found that teachers were needed in Israel, and he volunteered to teach high school biology. He was there one year, returned to the United States, received his master's degree in journalism, and went to work as a newspaper syndicated feature writer for United Feature Syndicate. (There are five major syndicates. Look at the small print at the beginning or end of stories in your local newspaper and you'll see if an article, editorial, or comic strip is syndicated.)

Hendin was a syndicated feature writer for 10 years, covering health, science, and the environment. When the first Earth Day was celebrated, Hendin wrote many columns about what was happening across the country. Environmental issues became more and more important, and Hendin was involved in bringing those stories to the American public. He also wrote about many medical advances during his journalistic career.

FROM WRITER TO MANAGER

Hendin moved into the management side of United Feature Syndicate and advanced to the positions of president of the book publishing division and senior vice president of the newspaper syndicate. While in those positions, he learned the art of negotiating contracts and had the opportunity to syndicate numerous famous comic strips and columnists.

GARFIELD WHO?

That crazy cat Garfield is in the comics partly because of Hendin. He syndicated the comic strip. Where would the world of business be without Dilbert? Hendin also signed that strip. And how good are your manners? Read "Miss Manners" (Judith Martin) to see how you're doing! That column was also syndicated by Hendin. At the time he signed "Miss Manners," there were no real etiquette columns in newspapers, and people said it wouldn't work. "Garfield" and "Dilbert" were not big successes in the beginning either. But look how popular they are now.

OUT ON HIS OWN

Hendin left the newspaper and book publishing company and started his own literary agency. The experience he gained during his career in the syndication business was invaluable in his new venture.

Now Hendin works with writers and artists to help them develop their work and market it to publishers or newspaper syndicates. He represents writers and cartoonists and deals in both fiction and nonfiction. He has some 50 clients. Judith Martin (Miss Manners) happens to be one of them. He also represents Guy and Brad Gilchrist, the creators of the "Nancy and Sluggo" cartoon strip. Dr. Abraham Twerski, a rabbi and psychologist who writes inspirational and self-help books, is also a client.

A FEW WORDS OF ADVICE

Hendin's advice for anyone who wants to enter the writing field is simple. He says, "Read a lot; write a lot. Read some more; write some more. Do interesting things and then write about them."

Hendin says that, throughout life, things always happen when least expected. If something is not an immediate success, stick to it, and you may be surprised at how successful it might be later on. Remember Garfield, Dilbert, and Miss Manners. . . .

Paralegal

SKILL SET

- ✔ COMPUTERS
- ✔ WRITING
- ✔ ADVENTURE

SHORTCUTS

GO visit your state legislature to see how laws are made.

READ John Grisham's books *The Rainmaker* (New York: Doubleday, 1995) or *The Firm* (New York: Doubleday, 1991). Both books feature some rather colorful paralegal talent.

TRY following news coverage of a big legal battle.

WHAT IS A PARALEGAL?

Paralegals, or legal assistants, work with lawyers to prepare information for legal cases. Paralegals research relevant information, organize facts and materials, and prepare comprehensive reports that are used by lawyers to prepare for lawsuits, trials, and other legal actions. In addition, more experienced paralegals may help prepare legal arguments, draft pleadings and motions to be filed in court, obtain affidavits, and assist lawyers in other ways. In fact, paralegals do many of the same types of tasks that lawyers do with a few notable exceptions. Paralegals cannot set legal fees, they cannot offer legal advice, and they cannot try cases in court.

Paralegal work requires an ability to conduct thorough research and to communicate the findings in a professional, organized way. As these documents can be very complex, paralegals must use good judgment in deciding how much information should be included in order to give a complete representation of the issue being explored. In addition to using law libraries, paralegals also use on-line legal research databases to make sure that they fully investigate every bit of information that might be relevant to a case. Speaking of investigation, paralegals often must get pretty creative in finding ways to track down all the facts in a case.

There are several ways to obtain the training needed to become a paralegal. Many colleges and universities offer two- to four-year paralegal programs that result in earning either an associate's degree or bachelor's degree. There are also certification courses that can be earned in a matter of months. This flexibility allows for some creative career-building options. For instance, one person may earn a four-year liberal arts degree followed by earning a paralegal certificate. Another may choose to earn the certificate first, get experience in the legal profession, and pursue additional education later. Others start working in a law office as a clerk or legal secretary and are promoted as they gain the necessary on-the-job training and experience. Some paralegals even go on to become lawyers.

Although it is not an absolute requirement, some paralegals find it to their advantage to become certified either by the National Association of Legal Assistants or the National Federation of Paralegal Associations. As in other careers, making a commitment to professionalism and learning as much as possible can only help advance your career.

Paralegals may specialize in a particular type of law such as corporate law, criminal law, sports and entertainment law, constitutional law, or environmental law. They may work for attorneys in large legal firms or small law offices as well as for government and community service agencies. Legal departments in corporations also hire paralegals. A paralegal career offers the opportunity to gain valuable technical writing skills while working in a very professional and highly specialized field.

TRY IT OUT

GET STUCK IN THE MIDDLE

Many schools organize peer mediation programs where students are trained to help other students work out disagreements. This can be an excellent way to experience justice in action. Talk to your school counselor or student council sponsor about peer mediation programs in your school district.

TRACK DOWN A LAW

Pick a legislative issue, something you are really interested in. Or better yet, pick an issue that is so obscure that it is hard to imagine why anyone would bother making a law about it. Contact your city, state, or national representative and ask for information about the bill. Make sure to obtain a copy of the proposed legislation itself (the language used in most legislative bills provides an excellent introduction to legal jargon, otherwise known as "legalese").

Follow the story in the newspaper to see what happens. Make a timeline to reflect its "life" until it is either passed into law or killed on the floor.

SPEND THE DAY IN COURT

The next time you have a day off from school, make arrangements to sit in on the proceedings in a courtroom. Whether it's juvenile court, traffic court, or the site of a major legal proceeding, it's sure to be an eye-opening experience.

INVESTIGATE THE OPTIONS

Before you decide about a paralegal career, find out all you can about your options. There are two main ways to research this information: at the library and on a computer. At the library, look for a book by Barbara Bernardo entitled *Paralegal: An Insider's Guide to One of the Fastest-Growing Occupations of the 1990s* (New York: Peterson's Guides, 1993). On the computer, visit the National Federation of Paralegal Associations' website at http://www.paralegals.org.

CHECK IT OUT

American Association for
Paralegal Education
P.O. Box 40244
Overland Park, Kansas 66204

American Bar Association
750 North Lake Shore Drive
Chicago, Illinois 60611

National Association of
Legal Assistants
1601 South Main Street, Suite 300
Tulsa, Oklahoma 74119

National Federation of
Paralegal Associations
104 Wilmot Road, Suite 201
Deerfield, Illinois 60015

National Paralegal Association
P.O. Box 406
Salsbury, Pennsylvania 18963

GET ACQUAINTED

Kimberle English, Paralegal

CAREER PATH

CHILDHOOD ASPIRATION: To be a flight attendant.

FIRST JOB: Working at a women's clothes store.

CURRENT JOB: Paralegal for a small law firm specializing in personal injury and family law.

A FEW DETOURS ALONG THE WAY

When Kimberle English was in high school, she got involved with Distributive Education Clubs of America (DECA). In this program, she and several of her friends had fun learning about real life and various careers. In the process, she discovered that she had a real interest in the law. After she graduated, she enrolled in a community college with every intention of going on to law school and becoming an attorney. Two years later she had earned an associate's degree, but her plan got left behind when she got married and had two children.

As it turns out, her husband left soon after the second child was born. English found herself with two children, few job skills, and no means of support for her young family. English soon found herself homeless and had to depend on public assistance to get through that tough period in her life.

Fortunately, she still had the desire to go into the legal profession, but with two children to raise and support, several years of law school was out of the question. She found, however, that the associate's degree she'd earned earlier served her well when she enrolled in a training program for paralegals. English was able to skip several courses by passing some tests and managed to finish the two-year program in a little more than a year.

A FRESH START

One of English's professors recommended her to a placement firm that specialized in paralegal work. Since she had graduated at the top of the class, English had no trouble finding lawyers who were willing to assign temporary special projects to her. Sometimes the work was as simple as transcribing dictation tapes (lots of typing!) or filing. One project required her to organize hundreds of boxes of documents for a huge court case involving the firm.

English worked in various law firms on a temporary basis until one offered her a full-time position. She eventually moved into her present position and really enjoys the opportunity to work on some of the more challenging aspects of paralegal work.

THE THRILL OF THE CHASE

English says that her favorite part of the job is the research. Each case is different, and she enjoys seeking out all the relevant information she can find. She finds that giving careful attention to every detail pays off, and she takes satisfaction in knowing that the result of her meticulous preparation can help clients win their legal battles.

THE COMMA LADY

No offense intended, but English has discovered that most attorneys need help expressing themselves. The attorneys she works with have come to rely on her command of grammar, punctuation, and other basics of written communication to make their sometimes brilliant legal insights read intelligently. One of the grammatically challenged lawyers has dubbed her "the comma lady."

This is another aspect of the work that English particularly enjoys. She says that taking the time to prepare accurate and well-written documents can make a difference in how a judge responds to a motion. Judges tend to get cranky about receiving sloppy, careless work from attorneys. They appreciate it when attorneys make the judge's job easier by expressing themselves clearly and concisely. English's behind-the-scenes work with a red pen and dictionary helps protect her bosses' reputation in the courtroom!

A HAPPY ENDING

Even though her original career ambitions got derailed by life's circumstances, English says that paralegal work is the best choice for her right now. She's still busy raising her children and would find it difficult to juggle being a single mother with all the responsibilities of being a lawyer. For now, being a paralegal offers the best of both worlds. She does much of the same kinds of interesting work that lawyers do, but she is able to sleep better at night knowing that the attorney has the ultimate responsibility.

Publicist

SKILL SET

- ✔ ADVENTURE
- ✔ TALKING
- ✔ WRITING

SHORTCUTS

GO to the movies, a concert, or a sports event and take note of all the promotional materials that are used to set the tone and bring in an audience.

READ the feature section of a major newspaper. You can bet that many of the articles about celebrities and new products got there as a result of a publicist's creative efforts.

TRY helping promote the next school prom or football game.

WHAT IS A PUBLICIST?

Having one's own publicist is the one thing that every big rock star, actor, author, pro athlete, and politician have in common. Publicists are public relations specialists who work to keep their clients' names in the news. Of course, it is generally preferred that their clients' names be associated with good news. But, a skilled publicist will know how to put a positive spin on the worst of circumstances as well.

Publicists help their famous clients stay famous by working with the media to keep them informed about noteworthy (or at least interesting) events. They do this by sending press releases and kits to carefully selected media people. Perhaps most important, they do it by maintaining friendly relationships with these people. This is a career in which what you know may be important but who you know is crucial. The most successful publicists take the time to nurture good relationships and earn the trust of the people who report the news by dealing with them professionally and with integrity.

Publicists may work for a public relations firm, a publishing house, a film studio, a major corporation, or a sports teams. Publicists with experience and good contacts are just as likely

to work independently, setting up their own business and representing any number of clients. They plan and implement publicity campaigns to get media attention for their clients.

While the work can be as varied as the personalities that publicists represent, there are several tasks that characterize the profession. For instance, you can count on publicists having a comprehensive press kit and media file for each of their clients. The press kit would include some basic ingredients such as a brief biography, photographs, and news clips about the client. Press kits are sent out along with a press release whenever there is a major event such as the release of a new movie or book or as part of a publicity campaign. Key to getting the coverage that's desired is writing effective press releases that, while subtlely self-serving, contain information an audience would want. Television and radio talk shows are other media sources that publicists work with to schedule spots for their clients.

In addition to actively seeking media coverage, a publicist may also handle inquiries from the media as a spokesperson for clients. This is particularly true in times of trouble when the publicist will work with the client to prepare a statement that represents the client's views on a matter and provide it to the media. This can be a useful way to satisfy curiosity while helping to maintain at least a semblance of privacy for the client.

Publicists may also arrange news conferences for clients to talk directly with the press, schedule private interviews with specific reporters, arrange photo opportunities for the press to get pictures of their clients, and plan special events such as opening night parties to gain added exposure for their clients. Media files are kept to track the success of publicity campaigns, and they contain clippings about their clients from newspapers and magazines all over the world. To keep a client or a job, publicists must prove their effectiveness by consistently getting their client's name in print or over the airwaves. Of course, all of these activities require very detailed planning and coordination with reporters. That part of the job keeps publicists busy on the phone.

If the publicist works for a publishing house or represents a notable author, he or she may also be responsible for scheduling author tours. This can be a rather complex undertaking that involves setting up interviews and special events in several cities across the country. The publicist is often responsible for planning the entire itinerary down to the smallest detail—including travel, lodging, and arranging for special meals. And the publicist's work begins long before the author arrives in a given city because the publicist must create an awareness of the authors and their latest books prior to the visit. One important part of this process is sending out review copies to book reviewers and feature writers of carefully selected newspapers and other appropriate publications.

Publicity is sought by any business to keep its name and products in full view of the buying public. Public relations is generally an important part of a company's overall marketing strategy. Think about it. Can you imagine how much it would cost to buy space to advertise your business on the front page of a national newspaper? Forget the specifics—you can be sure that it would cost a lot. What if you could get that space for the cost of a postage stamp and a few sheets of paper for a press release? Now you know why publicity and the people who know how to get it can be so valuable.

Publicists generally have earned a college degree in a field such as communications, public relations, journalism, or business. Seldom, if ever, do they start their careers by representing big Hollywood stars. Instead, they begin by working in a public relations firm or publishing house, photocopying and stuffing envelopes, while they learn techniques and perfect their skills.

TRY IT OUT

CLUB PR

Be on the lookout for groups in your school that could use some good public relations (PR)—maybe a sports team or an after-school club. Think of some newsworthy nugget of information and prepare a press kit to submit to the school or community newspaper. Perhaps your school band just got new uniforms or someone on the cross-country team broke a school record at the last meet.

Whatever the news, here are some things to include in your press kit: a press release that has a catchy headline, an interesting "hook" to get the reader interested in the story, and enough details to answer the who, what, where, when, why, and how questions that inquiring reporters everywhere will want answered; photographs of the event or the people featured in the story; and any other background materials that would make it easy for the newspaper editor to run your story in the next edition.

A VOTE FOR PUBLICITY

School elections are another good place to put your skills as a publicist to the test. Volunteer to help a candidate spread the word out about his or her campaign. Start by drawing up a plan that includes all the ideas you can think of for getting out the vote in the candidate's favor. Look at all the resources—publicity materials such as posters, special events that he or she can participate in, and other means to present his or her platform.

If you find that you enjoy the political process, don't stop with school elections. Volunteer to help work on any local campaign. Anyone running for public office—from a town council member to president of the United States—needs publicity. Find out how you can help get the word out about a good candidate.

FREE ADVERTISING

The Internet is the newest frontier for businesses looking to promote themselves. Here you'll find plenty of outright selling of goods, but if you look close enough, you'll also see some more subtle selling of a corporate image. Companies of all sizes are finding the Internet to be an effective way to promote their businesses with the type of information and activities that is the mainstay of good publicity. Quite often, companies gain name recognition by providing a useful service on-line. See for yourself how effective this public relations strategy can be by visiting the following sites.

http://www.gap.com
http://www.hersheys.com
http://www.universalstudios.com
http://www.disney.com
http://www.reebok.com

CHECK IT OUT

Publisher's Publicity Association
c/o Farrar, Straus & Giroux
19 Union Square West
New York, New York 10003

Publisher's Marketing Association
2401 Pacific Coast Highway, Suite 102
Hermosa Beach, California 90254

GET ACQUAINTED

Ann Flower, Publicist

CAREER PATH

CHILDHOOD ASPIRATION: To be an ecologist or start her own business.

FIRST JOB: Curatorial assistant in an art gallery.

CURRENT JOB: President of Ann Flower Communications.

EXPERIENCE COUNTS

Ann Flower is the daughter of two artists. Her only sister is an artist too. She says it seemed as though her parents and her sister were born knowing what to do. Their talents were recognized very early, so they went to art school and became artists. It wasn't so easy for Flower. She had many interests, could do several things fairly well, and was what you might call a "jack of all trades."

After Flower graduated from high school, she went to Europe to school for a year and liked it so well that she stayed for a while just to goof off and see the world. She came back to the United States and continued her schooling for a couple of years before taking off for Australia, where she had a job working for an American company. She then proceeded to work in a variety of fascinating jobs that prepared her for the work she is doing now.

There's a lesson to be learned from Flower's story. She admits, with a bit of hesitation, the she never finished her college education. On one hand, she regrets it. On the other hand, all the experience she gained from traveling and working helped prepare her for the work she's doing now. There are some things you can't learn in a book, and it turns out that her varied interests and talents were exactly what she needed to succeed as a public relations professional. Of course, she is quick to point out that her approach was unusual and wouldn't work for everyone.

AN ACCIDENTAL ENCOUNTER WITH PR

Flower found a career in public relations as a result of working as an assistant for a television producer. He told her about a job opening for a nonprofit organization called AmFAR (American Foundation for AIDS Research). She was intrigued by the idea of giving something back to the world, so she applied for the job and was hired to help organize fund-raising events. The job involved working with various public relations agencies to stage and publicize the events. That's where she discovered that public relations was a profession that really fit her eclectic background.

HOBNOBBING WITH CELEBRITIES

Her next career stop was handling public relations at a hotel in Santa Monica, California. Then she moved on to what she calls the ultimate hotel PR job at the prestigious Beverly Wilshire Hotel in Los Angeles, the site for the movie *Pretty Woman.* She said the job was fascinating, exciting, and busy—very busy. It seemed as though everyone who was anyone walked through the doors of that hotel. She had the opportunity to meet famous movie stars such as the late Jimmy Stewart, Michael Jackson, and Elizabeth Taylor. She was most intrigued by all the world leaders who came her way including Nelson Mandela, Margaret Thatcher, Hillary Clinton, George and Barbara Bush, and Sarah Ferguson.

ON HER OWN

Flower's expertise in hotel public relations landed her a position as vice president of the hospitality division for a public relations firm. She worked with a variety of clients until a few of her favorites talked her into starting her own agency so that she could give them more of her time.

She now handles publicity for clients as diverse as exclusive beauty salons, a company that makes upscale baby clothes, a home furnishings manufacturer, and a trendy restaurant chain. As different as the clients may be, her goal for all of them is the same: to find creative ways to expose them and their products to consumers. Achieving this goal may involve anything from having photographs of the client's products used in a magazine article to arranging a profile about the charitable activities of one of her clients.

VIRTUES OF THE SUCCESSFUL PUBLICIST

Flower says that you need two things to succeed in public relations: energy (lots of it) and patience (tons of it). When you are working for high-profile clients, the pace can run you ragged with the phone ringing constantly and events, interviews, and photo shots keeping you hopping. It takes a high level of energy to keep up.

Patience comes into play with the realization that good publicity doesn't come overnight. Flower says that it has taken up to a year to get some of her story ideas in print. Patience has paid off for Flower with major hits in publications such as *People* magazine, *USA Today*, and the *New York Times*. Publications like this get her clients' names in front of millions of people—making it well worth the wait.

Talk Show Producer

SKILL SET

- ✔ ADVENTURE
- ✔ TALKING
- ✔ WRITING

SHORTCUTS

GO sit in the audience of a television or radio talk show and watch how a show comes together.

READ an issue or two of *Teen People* for the latest news on hot celebrities. This magazine is available at local newsstands, bookstores, and libraries.

TRY making a list of ideas that would be interesting to discuss in a talk show format.

WHAT IS A TALK SHOW PRODUCER?

A talk show producer's work is quite similar to a newspaper or magazine editor's work. They are responsible for putting together an interesting variety of stories and information in a limited amount of space. There are three notable differences, however.

First, a talk show producer works with time limitations as opposed to space limitations. A talk show may consist of as much as an hour of airtime or as little as a five-second sound bite. Another difference is that although a talk show producer starts with written stories and pictures much like a newspaper editor, he or she must also work with the added dimensions of voices, personalities, and in the case of television, cameras and three-dimensional, moving graphics. The final difference, and it can be a big one, is that a talk show producer's work is often broadcast before a live audience. Producers don't have the luxury of editing their words and fixing mistakes. It's all there in living color!

All these ingredients make for a fast-paced and stimulating work environment that is ideal for writers who have lots of creative ideas, can think fast on their feet, and can make sound decisions about what's news and what's not. Good taste in developing stories that are appropriate for the general public's

viewing is another increasingly appreciated skill for talk show producers.

As you might expect, writing for a talk show can be quite different from writing for other formats. The copy must be concise, lively, and easily communicated verbally. Scripts must be tight and writers must consistently meet the challenge of effectively condensing major newsworthy events into 10- to 20-second stories.

Depending on the format of a show, a producer may be responsible for writing stories and putting together shows about the day's news, special edition news digests, documentaries about topics of interest to broad viewing audiences, promotional spots, and/or interviews with celebrities and other news-makers.

In addition to producing television and radio talk shows, talented writers may find opportunity in the growing audio book publishing industry. Here a producer must condense popular fiction or nonfiction books by about 60 percent so that the book can be read within the two- or three-hour timeframe that is standard for such products. The trick is that this must be achieved without sacrificing any of the most important aspects of the book—the characters, plot, setting—or the natural "voice" of the original book. It requires a process that goes a lot like this: Read the book, reread the book, write, cut, rewrite, cut, reread, cut some more, and so on.

Writers who want to produce television or radio talk shows or audio books would be well served by good training in a field such as broadcast journalism or communications. A college degree and experience at any level are helpful keys for getting started. More opportunities are to be found at smaller stations in smaller cities. Assignments for shows such as *The Rosie O'Donnell Show* and *Good Morning America* go to producers and writers who have proven themselves in smaller arenas and gained the skills and professional savvy necessary for making it in the big time.

TRY IT OUT

LIVE AT SIX

Take a typical day at school and make a list of all the noteworthy events. Go through the list and choose the five most important events. Write a news report that includes these stories in order of importance. Keep the language clear and concise but make sure the story highlights the most important aspects of the event. Your coverage should be complete enough that anyone could understand the significance of the story. Don't forget the weather and sports!

CUT TO THE CHASE

Pick a chapter from a favorite book, or find a good children's book—something interesting and of reasonable length. Your job is to rewrite the chapter or book, cutting it by at least 25 percent so that it can read as a book on tape. See what you can do to tighten things up without losing the original flavor and intent of the book's author. When you've finished, read the results into a tape recorder. Play the tape and see what you think.

For some professional feedback, visit the Audio Publisher's Association website at http://www.audiobooks.com.

NEWS IN A NUTSHELL

Listen to the evening news for an introduction to the skill of writing sound bites. Sound bites are quotes or explanations that somehow manage to conceptualize an entire subject or event in a matter of seconds. Good sound bites may be brief, but they are packed with memorable information. Politicians tend to be highly skilled in the art of sound bites. Pay attention to the way they describe legislative bills or issues on the newscast.

Now, think about something that has happened recently at school or in your community. See if you can come up with a clever sentence or two to explain it.

PRODUCER FOR A DAY

Pretend that you are the producer of your favorite television or radio talk show. Rosie O'Donnell? Paul Harvey? David Letterman? The line-up for tonight's show has completely fallen apart. You have to come up with a new show—now! Think of what topics and guests you'd put together for an entertaining show.

Get some ideas by checking out the actual line-ups of some of your favorite talk shows. Here are some web addresses for starters.

Find Jay Leno at http://www.nbc.com/tonightshow.
Find David Letterman at http://marketing.cbs.com/latenight/lateshow.
Find Rosie O'Donnell at http://www.rosieodonnell.com.
Find Oprah Winfrey at http://www.oprah.com.

CHECK IT OUT

Audio Publisher's Association
627 Aviation Way
Manhattan Beach, California 90266

Producer's Guild of America
400 South Beverly Drive, Room 211
Beverly Hills, California 90212

Recording Industry Association of America
1020 19th Street NW, Suite 200
Washington, D.C. 20036

Society of Professional Audio Recording Studios
4300 Tenth Avenue North
Lake Worth, Florida 33461

Women in Film
6464 Sunset Boulevard, Suite 660
Hollywood, California 90028

GET ACQUAINTED

Tom Giesen, Television Producer

CAREER PATH

CHILDHOOD ASPIRATION: To be a writer.

FIRST JOB: Dishwasher at The Bum Steer in Waterloo, Iowa.

CURRENT JOB: Freelance television producer and writer.

GO FOR THE GOAL

Ever since seeing the movie *All the President's Men* at the age of 13, Tom Giesen wanted to be a reporter. He attended parochial schools in Iowa and graduated from the University of Iowa with a degree in journalism. He also took television production classes and participated in theater productions.

LEARNING THE ROPES

Even though Giesen thought he wanted to be a television reporter, he decided that he had "more of a face for radio." He moved to Bloomington, Indiana, where he was hired to do on-air promotions in a small television market. He did a little bit of everything—from writing and creating graphics to producing and appearing on the air. Getting the chance to do it all showed him that he really liked writing and working behind the scenes best.

One of the funniest things that happened to Giesen during his stint in Indiana was being upstaged by a pig while working a show called *Live from the Monroe County Fair.* He was interviewing a young 4-H girl who had shown the prize pig. The pig liked plastic and wrapped himself in the microphone cord and took the microphone from Giesen. The pig finally dropped the microphone and the show went on!

ON TO BIGGER AND BETTER THINGS

Giesen moved on to Minnesota where he was a television news editor with the working hours of midnight to 9:00 A.M. (That doesn't do much for one's social life, does it?) He produced *Good Company,* a very popular talk show hosted by a husband and wife team and similar to *Regis and Kathie Lee.* At the time, *Good Company* was the highest rated local show in the country. The success of that show resulted in a call from a major television station in Colorado.

NEXT ON THE AGENDA

Giesen became writer and producer for *Good Afternoon, Colorado,* another very popular news and talk show. He was producer of that show for two years. During one of the shows, author Tony Hillerman's book *Sacred Clowns* was being reviewed. Giesen was in charge of the TelePrompTer (that's what the TV personality reads from). He accidentally wrote *Scared Clowns* rather than *Sacred Clowns.* Hillerman had fun kidding Giesen on air—something Giesen hasn't forgotten yet!

ON A ROLL

Finally, the more creative end of television beckoned, and Giesen has been a freelance writer and producer for the past several years. He has produced a crafts and antiques show for the Discovery Channel and 200 four-minute features for Discovery. He has written and produced business shows that aired on the Knowledge TV channel and several kids' shows. One, a show about video games, called *Twitch,* was very popular.

IN THE WORKS

Giesen is working on a 15-show schedule of *Ski World* which is shown three times a week on ESPN. The show is part travelogue and part skiing. A crew follows the United States ski team around the country. Giesen does the writing. The shooting of film is done in various locations. Then the material is sent to Giesen who assembles the shows for television.

Shows have featured skiers such as Picabo Street, Tommy Moe, and other nationally known skiers. A show has also been done on former president Jimmy Carter's program to teach underprivileged kids how to ski.

JUST WRITE IT

Giesen says if you want to write, you need to understand grammar and "be a great speller" (even when you have spell check on your computer). He believes in a casual style of writing, that is, writing the way people talk. Engage people with your writing, and help them understand your message. They need to "hear" what you're saying. Be interesting, be funny, and always meet your deadlines!

If you like to write, get involved in your school newspaper or yearbook production. Write as much as you can. Write so that people want to read or listen to what you write.

MAKE A WRITING DETOUR!

It's pretty amazing to think about all the ways you could put your interest in writing to work. The following lists include dozens of writing careers, and they barely scratch the surface of all the possibilities. These ideas are loosely grouped in categories to help you narrow down specific interest areas. Use them as a starting point to search out the best spot for your interests and abilities.

To make the most of this phase of your exploration, draw up a list of the ideas that you'd like to learn more about. Chances are there are at least three you've never heard of before. Look them up in a career encyclopedia and get acquainted with more possibilities for your future!

When you come across a particularly intriguing occupation, use the form on page 135 to record your discoveries.

A WORLD OF WRITING CAREERS

Write your way to success in some of the following careers.

A WAY WITH WORDS

These careers are for wordsmiths who have something to say and know how to say it.

cartoonist
catalog copywriter
children's book author
freelance writer
ghostwriter
greeting card writer
headline writer
journalist
newspaper columnist
novelist
poet
playwright
screenwriter
speechwriter
textbook writer
technical writer
television series writer
travel writer

THE BIG PICTURE

These careers require an ear for good and powerful language and a knack for managing the many details associated with producing books and other media products. A flair for writing in ways suitable to specific types of projects is also essential.

acquisitions editor
audio book producer
CD-ROM editor
children's book editor
computer game designer
database editor
desktop publisher
educational software editor
electronic publication specialist
encyclopedia editor
features editor
magazine editor
multimedia producer
on-line editor
TV producer
webmaster

NITTY-GRITTY DETAILS

People who do the following jobs often save other writers from seeing their embarrassing mistakes in print. These jobs involve some of the "quality assurance" aspects of writing and publishing.

abstractor
copy editor
dictionary editor
grammarian
indexer
proofreader
researcher

FAST AND FURIOUS

Tight deadlines and fast-paced writing demands are common ingredients of the following career ideas.

assignment editor
bureau chief
city editor
news anchor
news service correspondent
press secretary
public information officer
radio newscaster
reporter
stringer
wire service correspondent

IN OTHER WORDS

Teaching, analyzing, critiquing, or interpreting other people's writing is central to the following careers.

book reviewer
book buyer
critic
English teacher
English as a Second Language (ESL) teacher
journalism teacher
translator

IN THE WORD BUSINESS

While writing is only a part of the following occupations, it plays a big part, and good writing and communication skills are essential for success in these fields.

communications consultant
community affairs director
consumer affairs specialist
corporate communications director
development director
employee publication specialist
fund-raiser
investor relations specialist
marketing manager
media buyer
media planner
nonprofit organization administrator
promotions manager
publicist
recruiter

INFORMATION IS POWER

Mind-boggling, isn't it? There are so many great choices, so many jobs you've never heard of before. How will you ever narrow it down to the perfect spot for you?

First, pinpoint the ideas that sound the most interesting to you. Then, find out all you can about them.

As you may have noticed, a similar pattern of information was used for each of the career entries featured in this book. Each entry included

- a general description or definition of the career
- some hands-on projects that give readers a chance to actually experience a job
- a list of organizations to contact for more information
- an interview with a professional

You can use information like this to help you determine the best career path to pursue. Since there isn't room in one book to profile all these writing-related career choices, here's your chance to do it yourself. Conduct a full investigation into a writing career that interests you.

Please Note: If this book does not belong to you use a separate sheet of paper to record your responses to the following questions.

CAREER TITLE ______________________________

WHAT IS A ______________________________ **?**

Use career encyclopedias and other resources to write a description of this career.

____
____
____

SKILL SET

✔ ____________
✔ ____________
✔ ____________

TRY IT OUT

Write project ideas here. Ask your parents and your teacher to come up with a plan.

____
____
____

CHECK IT OUT

List professional organizations where you can learn more about this profession.

____
____
____

GET ACQUAINTED

Interview a professional in the field and summarize your findings.

____
____
____

DON'T STOP NOW!

GO FOR IT!

It's been a fast-paced trip so far. Take a break, regroup, and look at all the progress you've made.

1st Stop: Self-Discovery
You discovered some personal interests and natural abilities that you can start building a career around.

2nd Stop: Exploration
You've explored an exciting array of career opportunities in writing. You're now aware that your career can involve either a specialized area with many educational requirements or that it can involve a practical application of writing skills with a minimum of training and experience.

At this point, you've found a couple of (or few) careers that really intrigue you. Now it's time to put it all together and do all you can to make an informed, intelligent choice. It's time to move on.

3rd Stop: Experimentation

By the time you finish this section, you'll have reached one of three points in the career planning process.

1. **Green light!** You found it. No need to look any further. This is *the* career for you. (This may happen to a lucky few. Don't worry if it hasn't happened yet for you. This whole process is about exploring options, experimenting with ideas, and, eventually, making the best choice for you.)
2. **Yellow light!** Close, but not quite. You seem to be on the right path but you haven't nailed things down for sure. (This is where many people your age end up, and it's a good place to be. You've learned what it takes to really check things out. Hang in there. Your time will come.)
3. **Red light!** Whoa! No doubt about it, this career just isn't for you. (Congratulations! Aren't you glad you found out now and not after you'd spent four years in college preparing for this career? Your next stop: Make a U-turn and start this process over with another career.)

Here's a sneak peek at what you'll be doing in the next section.

- First, you'll pick a favorite career idea (or two or three).
- Second, you'll snoop around the library to find answers to the 10 things you've just got to know about your future career.
- Third, you'll pick up the phone and talk to someone whose career you admire to find out what it's really like.
- Fourth, you'll link up with a whole world of great information about your career idea on the Internet (it's easier than you think).
- Fifth, you'll go on the job to shadow a professional for a day.

Hang on to your hats and get ready to make tracks!

#1 NARROW DOWN YOUR CHOICES

You've been introduced to quite a few writing career ideas. You may also have some ideas of your own to add. Which ones appeal to you the most?

Write your top three choices in the spaces below. (Sorry if this is starting to sound like a broken record, but . . . if this book does not belong to you, write your responses on a separate sheet of paper.)

1. ______________________________
2. ______________________________
3. ______________________________

#2 SNOOP AT THE LIBRARY

Take your list of favorite career ideas, a notebook, and a helpful adult with you to the library. When you get there, go to the reference section and ask the librarian to help you find books about careers. Most libraries will have at least one set of career encyclopedias. Some of the larger libraries may also have career information on CD-ROM.

Gather all the information you can and use it to answer the following questions in your notebook about each of the careers on your list. Make sure to ask for help if you get stuck.

TOP 10 THINGS YOU NEED TO KNOW ABOUT YOUR CAREER

1. What kinds of skills does this job require?
2. What kind of training is required? (Compare the options for a high school degree, trade school degree, two-year degree, four-year degree, and advanced degree.)
3. What types of classes do I need to take in high school in order to be accepted into a training program?
4. What are the names of three schools or colleges where I can get the training I need?
5. Are there any apprenticeship or internship opportunities available? If so, where? If not, could I create my own opportunity? How?
6. How much money can I expect to earn as a beginner? How much with more experience?
7. What kinds of places hire people to do this kind of work?
8. What is a typical work environment like? For example, would I work in a busy office, outdoors, or in a laboratory?
9. What are some books and magazines I could read to learn more about this career? Make a list and look for them at your library.
10. Where can I write for more information? Make a list of professional associations.

#3 CHAT ON THE PHONE

Talking to a seasoned professional—someone who experiences the job day in and day out—can be a great way to get the inside story on what a career is all about. Fortunately for you, the experts in any career field can be as close as the nearest telephone.

Sure it can be a bit scary calling up an adult whom you don't know. But, two things are in your favor:

1. They can't see you. The worst thing they can do is hang up on you, so just relax and enjoy the conversation.
2. They'll probably be happy to talk to you about their job. In fact, most people will be flattered that you've called. If you happen to contact someone who seems reluctant to talk, thank them for their time and try someone else.

Here are a few pointers to help make your telephone interview a success.

- Mind your manners and speak clearly.
- Be respectful of their time and position.
- Be prepared with good questions and take notes as you talk.

One more common sense reminder: Be careful about giving out your address and DO NOT arrange to meet anyone you don't know without your parents' supervision.

TRACKING DOWN CAREER EXPERTS

You might be wondering by now how to find someone to interview. Have no fear! It's easy, if you're persistent. All you have to do is ask. Ask the right people and you'll have a great lead in no time.

A few of the people to ask and sources to turn to are

Your parents. They may know someone (or know someone who knows someone) who has just the kind of job you're looking for.

Your friends and neighbors. You might be surprised to find out how many interesting jobs these people have when you start asking them what they (or their parents) do for a living.

Librarians. Since you've already figured out what kinds of companies employ people in your field of interest, the next step is to ask for information about local employers. Although it's a bit cumbersome to use, a big volume called *Contacts Influential* can provide this kind of information.

Professional associations. Call or write to the professional associations you discovered in Activity #1 a few pages back and ask for recommendations.

Chambers of commerce. The local chamber of commerce probably has a directory of employers, their specialties, and their phone numbers. Call the chamber, explain what you are looking for, and give them a chance to help their future workforce.

Newspaper and magazine articles. Find an article about the subject you are interested in. Chances are pretty good that it will mention the name of at least one expert in the field. The article probably won't include the person's phone number (that would be too easy), so you'll have to look for clues. Common clues include the name of the company that they work for, the town that they live in, and if the person is an author, the name of their publisher. Make a few phone calls and track them down (if long distance calls are involved, make sure to get your parents' permission first).

INQUIRING KIDS WANT TO KNOW

Before you make the call, make a list of questions to ask. You'll cover more ground if you focus on using the five w's (and the h) that you've probably heard about in your creative writing classes: Who? What? Where? When? How? and Why? For example,

1. Who do you work for?
2. What is a typical work day like for you?
3. Where can I get some on-the-job experience?
4. When did you become a ______________________ ?
   (profession)
5. How much can you earn in this profession? (But, remember it's not polite to ask someone how much *he* or *she* earns.)
6. Why did you choose this profession?

One last suggestion: Add a professional (and very classy) touch to the interview process by following up with a thank-you note to the person who took time out of a busy schedule to talk with you.

#4 SURF THE NET

With the Internet, the new information superhighway, charging full steam ahead, you literally have a world of information at your fingertips. The Internet has something for everyone, and it's getting easier to access all the time. An increasing number of libraries and schools are offering access to the Internet on their computers. In addition, companies such as America Online and CompuServe have made it possible for anyone with a home computer to surf the World Wide Web.

A typical career search will land everything from the latest news on developments in the field and course notes from universities to museum exhibits, interactive games, educational activities, and more. You just can't beat the timeliness or the variety of information available on the Net.

One of the easiest ways to track down this information is to use an Internet search engine, such as Yahoo! Simply type in the topic you are looking for, and in a matter of seconds, you'll have a list of options from around the world. It's fun to browse—you never know what you'll come up with.

To narrow down your search a bit, look for specific websites, forums, or chatrooms that are related to your topic in the following publications:

Hahn, Harley. *The Internet Yellow Pages.* Berkeley, Calif.: Osborne McGraw Hill, 1997.

———. *The World Wide Web Yellow Pages.* Berkeley, Calif.: Osborne McGraw Hill, 1997.

To go on-line at home you may want to compare two of the more popular on-line services: America Online and CompuServe. Please note that there is a monthly subscription fee for using these services. There can also be extra fees attached to specific forums and services, so *make sure you have your parents' OK before you sign up.* For information about America Online call 800-827-6364. For information about CompuServe call 800-848-8990. Both services frequently offer free start-up deals, so shop around.

There are also many other services, depending on where you live. Check your local phone book or ads in local computer magazines for other service options.

Before you link up, keep in mind that many of these sites are geared toward professionals who are already working in a particular field. Some of the sites can get pretty technical. Just use the experience as a chance to nose around the field, hang out with the people who are tops in the field, and think about whether or not you'd like to be involved in a profession like that.

Specific sites to look for are the following:

Professional associations. Find out about what's happening in the field, conferences, journals, and other helpful tidbits.

Schools that specialize in this area. Many include research tools, introductory courses, and all kinds of interesting information.

Government agencies. Quite a few are going high-tech with lots of helpful resources.

Websites hosted by experts in the field (this seems to be a popular hobby among many professionals). These websites are often as entertaining as they are informative.

If you're not sure where to go, just start clicking around. Sites often link to other sites. You may want to jot down notes about favorite sites. Sometimes you can even print out information that isn't copyright-protected; try the print option and see what happens.

Be prepared: Surfing the Internet can be an addicting habit! There is so much great information. It's a fun way to focus on your future.

#5 SHADOW A PROFESSIONAL

Linking up with someone who is gainfully employed in a profession that you want to explore is a great way to find out what a career is like. Following someone around while the person is at work is called "shadowing." Try it!

This process involves three steps.

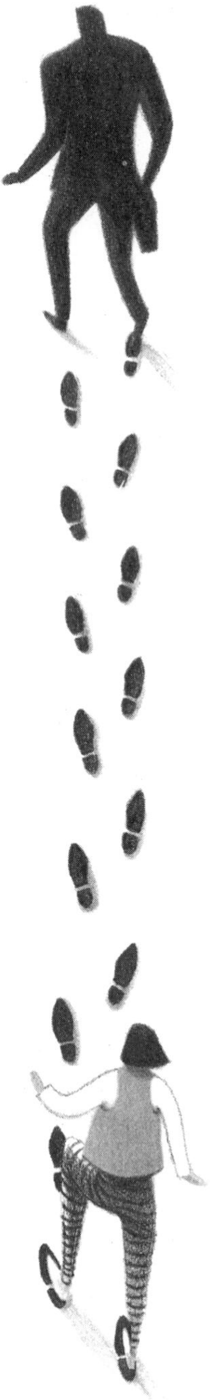

1. Find someone to shadow. Some suggestions include
   - the person you interviewed (if you enjoyed talking with him or her and feel comfortable about asking the person to show you around the workplace)
   - friends and neighbors (you may even be shocked to discover that your parents have interesting jobs)
   - workers at the chamber of commerce may know of mentoring programs available in your area (it's a popular concept, so most larger areas should have something going on)
   - someone at your local School-to-Work office, the local Boy Scouts Explorer program director (this is available to girls too), or your school guidance counselor
2. Make a date. Call and make an appointment. Find out when is the best time for arrival and departure. Make arrangements with a parent or other respected adult to go with you and get there on time.
3. Keep your ears and eyes open. This is one time when it is OK to be nosy. Ask questions. Notice everything that is happening around you. Ask your host to let you try some of the tasks he or she is doing.

The basic idea of the shadowing experience is to put yourself in the other person's shoes and see how they fit. Imagine yourself having a job like this 10 or 15 years down the road. It's a great way to find out if you are suited for a particular line of work.

BE CAREFUL OUT THERE!

Two cautions must accompany this recommendation. First, remember the stranger danger rules of your childhood. NEVER meet with anyone you don't know without your parents' permission and ALWAYS meet in a supervised situation—at the office or with your parents.

Second, be careful not to overdo it. These people are busy earning a living, so respect their time by limiting your contact and coming prepared with valid questions and background information.

PLAN B

If shadowing opportunities are limited where you live, try one of these approaches for learning the ropes from a professional.

Pen pals. Find a mentor who is willing to share information, send interesting materials, or answer specific questions that come up during your search.

Cyber pals. Go on-line in a forum or chatroom related to your profession. You'll be able to chat with professionals from all over the world.

If you want to get some more on-the-job experience, try one of these approaches.

Volunteer to do the dirty work. Volunteer to work for someone who has a job that interests you for a specified period of time. Do anything—filing, errands, emptying trash cans—that puts you in contact with professionals. Notice every tiny detail about the profession. Listen to the lingo they use in the profession. Watch how they perform their jobs on a day-to-day basis.

Be an apprentice. This centuries-old job training method is making a comeback. Find out if you can set up an official on-the-job training program to gain valuable experience. Ask professional associations about apprenticeship opportunities. Once again, a School-to-Work program can be a great asset. In many areas, they've established some very interesting career training opportunities.

Hire yourself for the job. Maybe you are simply too young to do much in the way of on-the-job training right now. That's OK. Start learning all you can now and you'll be ready to really wow them when the time is right. Make sure you do all the Try It Out activities included for the career(s) you are most interested in. Use those activities as a starting point for creating other projects that will give you a feel for what the job is like.

WHAT'S NEXT?

Have you carefully worked your way through all of the suggested activities? You haven't tried to sneak past anything, have you? This isn't a place for shortcuts. If you've done the activities, you're ready to decide where you stand with each career idea. So what is it? Green light? See page 152. Yellow light? See page 151. Red light? See page 150. Find the spot that best describes your response to what you've discovered about this career idea and plan your next move.

RED LIGHT

So you've decided this career is definitely not for you—hang in there! The process of elimination is an important one. You've learned some valuable career planning skills; use them to explore other ideas. In the meantime, use the following road map to chart a plan to get beyond this "spinning your wheels" point in the process.

Take a variety of classes at school to expose yourself to new ideas and expand the options. Make a list of courses you want to try.

- ______________________________
- ______________________________
- ______________________________
- ______________________________

Get involved in clubs and other after-school activities (like 4-H or Boy Scout Explorers) to further develop your interests. Write down some that interest you.

- ______________________________
- ______________________________
- ______________________________
- ______________________________

Read all you can find about interesting people and their work. Make a list of people you'd like to learn more about.

- ______________________________
- ______________________________
- ______________________________
- ______________________________

Keep at it. Time is on your side. Finding the perfect work for you is worth a little effort. Once you've crossed this hurdle, move on to the next pages and continue mapping out a great future.

YELLOW LIGHT

Proceed with caution. While the idea continues to intrigue you, you may wonder if it's the best choice for you. Your concerns are legitimate (listen to that nagging little voice inside!).

Maybe it's the training requirements that intimidate you. Maybe you have concerns about finding a good job once you complete the training. Maybe you wonder if you have what it takes to do the job.

At this point, it's good to remember that there is often more than one way to get somewhere. Check out all the choices and choose the route that's best for you. Use the following road map to move on down the road in your career planning adventure.

Make two lists. On the first, list the things you like most about the career you are currently investigating. On the second, list the things that are most important to you in a future career. Look for similarities on both lists and focus on careers that emphasize these similar key points.

Current Career	Future Career
____________________	____________________
____________________	____________________

What are some career ideas that are similar to the one you have in mind? Find out all you can about them. Go back through the exploration process explained on pages 139 to 148 and repeat some of the exercises that were most valuable.

- ____
- ____
- ____
- ____

Visit your school counselor and ask him or her which career assessment tools are available through your school. Use these to find out more about your strengths and interests. List the date, time, and place for any assessment tests you plan to take.

- ______________________________
- ______________________________
- ______________________________
- ______________________________

What other adults do you know and respect to whom you can talk about your future? They may have ideas that you've never thought of.

- ______________________________
- ______________________________
- ______________________________
- ______________________________

What kinds of part-time jobs, volunteer work, or after-school experiences can you look into that will give you a chance to build your skills and test your abilities? Think about how you can tap into these opportunities.

- ______________________________
- ______________________________
- ______________________________
- ______________________________

GREEN LIGHT

Yahoo! You are totally turned on to this career idea and ready to do whatever it takes to make it your life's work. Go for it!

Find out what kinds of classes you need to take now to prepare for this career. List them here.

- ______________________________
- ______________________________
- ______________________________
- ______________________________

What are some on-the-job training possibilities for you to pursue? List the company name, a person to contact, and the phone number.

- ______________________________
- ______________________________
- ______________________________
- ______________________________

Find out if there are any internship or apprenticeship opportunities available in this career field. List contacts and phone numbers.

- ______________________________
- ______________________________
- ______________________________
- ______________________________

What kind of education will you need after you graduate from high school? Describe the options.

- ______________________________
- ______________________________
- ______________________________
- ______________________________

No matter what the educational requirements are, the better your grades are during junior and senior high school, the better your chances for the future.

Take a minute to think about some areas that need improvement in your schoolwork. Write your goals for giving it all you've got here.

- ______________________________
- ______________________________
- ______________________________
- ______________________________

Where can you get the training you'll need? Make a list of colleges, technical schools, or vocational programs. Include addresses so that you can write to request a catalog.

- ______________________________
- ______________________________
- ______________________________
- ______________________________

HOORAY! YOU DID IT!

This has been quite a trip. If someone tries to tell you that this process is easy, don't believe it. Figuring out what you want to do with the rest of your life is heavy stuff, and it should be. If you don't put some thought (and some sweat and hard work) into the process, you'll get stuck with whatever comes your way. Make sure you make the most of your potential.

You may not have things planned to a T. Actually, it's probably better if you don't. You'll change some of your ideas as you grow and experience new things. And, you may find an interesting detour or two along the way. That's OK.

The most important thing about beginning this process now is that you've started to dream. You've discovered that you have some unique talents and abilities to share. You've become aware of some of the ways you can use them to make a living—and, perhaps, make a difference in the world.

Whatever you do, don't lose sight of the hopes and dreams you've discovered. You've got your entire future ahead of you. Use it wisely.

SOME FUTURE DESTINATIONS

Wow! You've really made tracks during this whole process. Now that you've gotten this far, you'll want to keep moving forward to a great future. This section will point you toward some useful resources to help you make a conscientious career choice (that's just the opposite of falling into any old job on a fluke).

IT'S NOT JUST FOR NERDS

The school counselor's office is not just a place where teachers send troublemakers. One of its main purposes is to help students like you make the most of your educational opportunities. Most schools will have a number of useful resources, including career assessment tools (ask about the Self-Directed Search Career Explorer or the COPS Interest

Inventory—these are especially useful assessments for people your age). There may also be a stash of books, videos, and other helpful materials.

Make sure no one's looking and sneak into your school counseling office to get some expert advice!

AWESOME INTERNET CAREER RESOURCES

Your parents will be green with envy when they see all the career planning resources you have at your fingertips. Get ready to hear them whine, "But they didn't have all this stuff when I was a kid." Make the most of these cyberspace opportunities.

- The Career Center for Teens (a site sponsored by Public Television Outreach) includes activities and information on 21st-century career opportunities. Find it at http://www.pbs.org/jobs/teenindex.html.
- Future Scan includes in-depth profiles on a wide variety of career choices and expert advice from their "Guidance Gurus." Check it out at http://www.futurescan.com.
- Just for fun visit the Jam!z Knowzone Careers page and chat with other kids about your career dreams. You'll find them by going to http://www.jamz.com and clicking on the KnowZone icon. (Note: This site is monitored!)
- JobSmart's Career Guides is another site to explore specific career choices. Look for it at http://www.jobsmart.org/tools/career/spec-car.htm.

IT'S NOT JUST FOR BOYS

Boys and girls alike are encouraged to contact their local version of the Boy Scouts Explorer program. It offers exciting on-the-job training experiences in a variety of professional fields. Look in the white pages of your community phone book for the local Boy Scouts of America program.

MORE CAREER BOOKS ESPECIALLY FOR WRITERS

There are a surprising number of ways to earn a living as a writer. The following books provide more information about additional career options for writers.

Camenson, Blythe. *Great Jobs for Communications Majors.* Lincolnwood, Ill.: VGM Career Horizons, 1995.

Careers Research Monographs. *Writing as a Career.* Chicago: Institute for Research, 1994.

Carter, Robert A. *Opportunities in Book Publishing Careers.* Lincolnwood, Ill: VGM Career Horizons, 1987.

DeGalan, Julie. *Great Jobs for English Majors.* Lincolnwood, Ill: VGM Career Horizons, 1994.

Eberts, Marjorie. *Careers for Bookworms and Other Literary Types.* Lincolnwood, Ill: VGM Career Horizons, 1995.

Ferguson, Donald L., and Jim Patten. *Opportunities in Journalism Careers.* Lincolnwood, Ill: VGM Career Horizons, 1993.

Foote-Smith, Elizabeth. *Opportunities in Writing Careers.* Lincolnwood, Ill.: VGM Career Horizons, 1990.

Goldberg, Jan. *Careers in Journalism.* Lincolnwood, Ill.: VGM Career Horizons, 1995.

———. *Real People Working in Communications.* Lincolnwood, Ill.: VGM Career Horizons, 1996.

Gould, J. R., and W. A. Losano. *Opportunities in Technical Writing and Communication Careers.* Lincolnwood, Ill.: VGM Career Horizons, 1994.

Guiley, Rosemary Ellen. *Career Opportunities for Writers.* New York: Facts On File, 1995.

Meyer, Scott A. *100 Jobs in Words.* New York: Macmillan, 1996.

Noronha, Shonan F. R. *Careers in Communications.* Lincolnwood, Ill.: VGM Career Horizons, 1994.

Pattis, William. *Opportunities in Magazine Publishing.* Lincolnwood, Ill.: VGM Career Horizons, 1992.

Van Wicklen, J. *The Technical Writing Game: A Complete Guide for Aspiring Writers.* New York: Facts On File, 1992.

HEAVY-DUTY RESOURCES

Career encyclopedias provide general information about a lot of professions and can be a great place to start a career search. Those listed here are easy to use and provide useful information about nearly a zillion different jobs. Look for them in the reference section of your local library.

Cosgrove, Holli, ed. *Career Discovery Encyclopedia: 1997 Edition.* Chicago: J. G. Ferguson Publishing Company, 1997.

Encyclopedia of Career Choices for the 1990's. New York: Perigee Books/Putnam Publishing Group, 1992.

Maze, Marilyn, Donald Mayall, and J. Michael Farr. *The Enhanced Guide for Occupational Exploration: Descriptions for the 2,500 Most Important Jobs.* Indianapolis: JIST, 1995

VGM's Careers Encyclopedia. Lincolnwood, Ill.: VGM Career Books, 1997.

FINDING PLACES TO WORK

Use resources like these to find leads on local businesses, mentors, job shadowing opportunities, and internships. Later, use these same resources to find a great job!

LeCompte, Michelle. *Job Hunter's Sourcebook: Where to Find Employment Leads and Other Job Search Resources.* Detroit: Gale Research Inc., 1996.

Morgan, Brad. *Book Publishing Career Directory.* Detroit: Gale Research, 1992.

Also consult the Job Bank series (Holbrook, Mass.: Adams Media Group). Adams publishes separate guides for Atlanta, Seattle, and many major points in between. Ask your local librarian if they have a guide for the biggest city near you.

FINDING PLACES TO PRACTICE JOB SKILLS

An apprenticeship is an official opportunity to learn a specific profession by working side by side with a skilled professional. As a training method, it's as old as the hills, and it's making a comeback in a big way because people are realizing that doing a job is simply the best way to learn a job.

An internship is an official opportunity to gain work experience (paid or unpaid) in an industry of interest. Interns are more likely to be given entry-level tasks but often have the chance to rub elbows with people in key positions within a company. In comparison to an apprenticeship, which offers very detailed training for a specific job, an internship offers a broader look at a particular kind of work environment.

Both are great ways to learn the ropes and stay one step ahead of the competition. Consider it dress rehearsal for the real thing!

Cantrell, Will. *International Internships and Volunteer Programs.* Oakton, Va.: World Wise Books, 1992.

Guide to Apprenticeship Programs for Non-College Bound Youth. New York: Rosen, 1996.

Hepburn, Diane, ed. *Internships 1997.* Princeton, N.J.: Peterson's, 1997.

Summerfield, Carol J., and Holli Cosgrove. *Ferguson's Guide to Apprenticeship Programs: Traditional and Nontraditional.* Chicago: Ferguson's, 1994.

NO-COLLEGE OCCUPATIONS

Some of you will be relieved to learn that a college degree is not the only route to a satisfying, well-paying career. Whew! If you'd rather skip some of the schooling and get down to work, here are some books you need to consult.

Abrams, Kathleen S. *Guide to Careers Without College.* Danbury, Conn.: Franklin Watts, 1995.

Corwen, Leonard, *College Not Required!: 100 Great Careers That Don't Require a College Degree.* New York: Macmillan, 1995.

Farr, J. Michael. *America's Top Jobs for People Without College Degrees.* Indianapolis: JIST, 1997.

Unger, Harlow G. *But What If I Don't Want to Go to College?: A Guide to Success through Alternative Education.* Rev. ed. New York: Facts On File, 1998.

INDEX

Page numbers in **boldface** indicate main articles. Page numbers in *italics* indicate photographs.